Probably the Best Niche List

7K+

Over 7 thousand niche categories to *spark* Ideas from

Kenny G. Foster

Copyright © 2017 Kenny G. Foster

All rights reserved.

ISBN: 1545402620
ISBN-13: 978-1545402627

A

- Advertising Traveling Signboards
- Architectural & Block Glass
- Aluminum Windows
- Animal Behavior Services
- Air & Gas Compressor
- Adult & Elderly Sitting Services
- Auto Trim
- Appliances
- Auto Upholstery Cleaning
- Agricultural Producers & Products
- Antiques Wholesale
- Audiovisual Equipment
- Archaeologists
- Adhesive & Glue Equipment
- Alcoholic Beverages
- Appliance Parts
- Aerospace Research & Development
- Antique Furniture Refinishing
- Acoustical Contractors
- Air Shows
- Aircraft & Aviation Insurance
- Adult Personals
- Auto Diagnostic Services
- Auto Salvage Yards

- Antique Dolls
- Air Cleaning & Purifying Services
- Auto Paint-less Dent Repair
- Amplifiers
- Attorneys' Support Services
- Audiovisual Equipment
- Animal Cages & Racks
- Accommodation & Reservations
- Asphalt & Asphalt Products
- Apartments
- Auto Radiator Repair & Rebuilding
- Auto Upholstery
- Auto Batteries
- Asbestos Testing Laboratories
- After School Programs
- Alternative Medicine
- Aircraft Manufacturers
- Airline Travel Agents
- Agricultural Consultants
- Abandoned Tank Filling
- Agricultural Research & Education
- Archery Ranges
- Air Quality Management Services
- Advertising Employment Agencies
- Audio Equipment
- Auto Wheels

- Awnings & Canopies
- Auto Inspection Equipment
- Auto Paint
- African Books
- Asset Protection Attorneys
- Artists & Art Studios
- Air Quality Measurement Equipment
- Art Installation Services
- Army & Navy Stores
- Abortion Information
- Advertising Searchlights
- Auto Alternators & Starters
- Acting Schools
- Air Conditioning
- Adhesive Tapes
- Anniversary Gifts
- Axles
- Auto Accessories
- Alternative Medicine Physicians & Surgeons
- Auto Body Parts
- Antique Paintings & Prints
- ATM Sales & Service
- Antiques Appraisers
- Architectural Sculptures
- Auto Service & Repair
- Auto Gas Tank Installation & Removal
- Asphalt Sealers
- Acupuncture & Acupressure Specialists

- Alzheimer's Information
- Abortion Clinics
- Amusement Park Rides & Equipment
- Appliance Installation & Hook-up
- Appliance Repair
- Auto Wrecking Information
- Addiction Information & Treatment
- African Art Galleries
- Asbestos & Lead Abatement & Removal Services
- Animal Control
- Apartment Sharing & Roommates
- Advertising Displays
- Anti-Aging Medicine Physicians & Surgeons
- Analytical Testing Laboratories
- Accident Reconstruction Services
- Aquarium Leasing & Maintenance
- Art Goods
- Appliance Painting & Refinishing
- Acoustical Ceiling Tiles
- Auto Electrical Systems Service & Repair
- Auto Registration, Tags & Titles
- Auto Financing & Loans

- Ammunition Reloading Equipment
- Auto Fleet Maintenance
- Art Consultants
- Aerobics Instruction
- Architectural Photographers
- Auto Appearance & Protection
- Accident Attorneys
- Auto Floor Coverings
- Animal Feed
- Acoustical Materials
- Auto Engine Balancing
- Audiometry
- Animated Signs & Displays
- Air & Gas Compressors
- Auto Inspection
- Auto Body Equipment
- Aircraft Radio Equipment
- Accommodations & Lodging
- Auto Washing & Polishing
- Artificial Stone & Brick
- Acupuncture Information
- Airline Flight Information
- Auto Licenses
- Auto & Truck
- Airplane Pilots
- Art Reproductions
- Accident Report Services
- ATV
- Assembly of God Churches
- Anesthesiology Physicians
- Art Distributors & Publishers
- Air Analysis Testing Laboratories
- Apartment Furnishings
- Air Cleaning & Purifying Equipment
- Autism Services
- Arbitration & Mediation Services
- Amusement Equipment
- Accident & Health Insurance
- Apprenticeships
- Asbestos Abatement & Removal Equipment
- Aircraft Management Services
- Auto Remote Starters
- Addressing Machines
- Automation & Control Systems Engineers
- Art Casting
- Air Conditioning Contractors
- Accounts Receivable Loans
- Aerial Photographers
- Alternative Medicine Practitioners
- Auto Race Track Equipment

- Art Wholesale
- Architectural Graphics
- Auto Cleaning
  & Detailing
- Air & Gas Filters
- Aquariums
- Accountants
  Employment Agencies
- ATV Tours
- Air Conditioning
  Cleaning
- Asbestos Removal
  - Residential
- Auto Suspension Parts
- Antique & Estate
  Jewelry
- Architectural Support
  Services
- Appeals Attorneys
- Auto Race Tracks
- Animal & Pet
  Photographers
- Air Boats
- Auto Purchasing
  Consultants
- African Restaurants
- Auto Glass Replacement
  & Repair
- Alterations
  & Tailoring
- Artificial Flowers
  & Trees
- Asbestos Inspection
- Advertising Production
  Services
- Adult Day Care Centers
- Aluminum Products

- Absorbents
- Auto Parts Warehouses
- Auto Warranty Services
- Amish Goods
  & Services
- Auto Locators
- Animal Rescue
  & Preservation Services
- Auto Engine Rebuilding
- Aerial Applicators
- Adult Entertainment
  Products & Services
- Artesian Well
  Contractors
- Advertising Layout
  & Design Printing
- Auto Towing Equipment
- Anglican Churches
- Arborists
- Agricultural Outdoor
  Power Equipment
- Assisted Living Facilities
- Auto Gas Tanks
- Adult Entertainment
  Nightclubs
- Adult Entertainment
  Comedy & Dance Clubs
- Auto Racing
- Auto Springs
- Auto Customizing,
  Conversion, &
  Restoration
- Aviation & Aerospace
  Medicine Physicians
  & Surgeons
- Advertising &
  Promotional Apparel

- Addiction Psychiatry Physicians
- Adoption Agencies & Services
- Auto Body Equipment Repair
- Answering Services
- Antenna Equipment & Service
- Auto Parts
- Animal Shelters
- Animal Shows & Organizations
- Accordions
- Asphalt & Road Oils
- Adhesive Labels
- Auto Title Loans
- Adjustment & Collection Services
- Auto & Truck Wrecking
- Auto Auctions
- Aircraft & Equipment Testing
- Auto Glass Coating & Tinting
- Agricultural Engineers
- Architects - Residential
- Advertising Balloons & Signage
- Archery Equipment
- Abuse Information
- Architectural Engineers
- Amusement & Theme Parks
- Agricultural Building Construction
- Antifreeze
- Antique Restoration Supplies & Hardware
- AIDS & HIV Treatment Centers
- Auto Radiators
- Archives, Records, & Documents Storage
- Auto Covers
- Audiologists
- Auto Transmissions
- Artificial Turf
- Acupuncture Physicians
- Auto Frames Service & Repair
- Audio & Video Recording Equipment
- Advertising & Display Posters
- Adobe Materials & Contractors
- Auto CV Joints & Axles
- Antiques & Collectibles
- Ambulance & Hearse Manufacturers
- Antique Reproductions
- Adult Care
- Asbestos Diseases Attorneys
- Audio Video Equipment Service & Repair
- Agricultural Laboratories
- Athletic & Dance Shoes
- Air Duct Cleaning
- Alarm Systems
- Animal Transport Services

- Auto Bumpers & Grills
- Architectural Planning Consultants
- Aluminum Manufacturers
- Afghan Restaurants
- Agricultural Seeds
- Auto Fuel Injection Service
- Asian Goods
- Aluminum Fences
- Adult & Continuing Education Seminars & Workshops
- Armenian Restaurants
- Alzheimer's Support Groups
- Asian Restaurants
- Animal Nutrition Consultants
- Architectural Drafting
- Antique & Classic Auto
- Auto Service Clubs
- Allergy Testing Laboratories
- Auto Equipment
- Aquariums
- Asphalt Pavement Repair
- Auto Buyers
- Art Galleries
- Accountants
- Aerial Advertising
- Advertising & Promotional Products
- Antique Watches

- Agricultural Seeding & Spraying
- Art Appraisers
- Alignment, Frame, & Axle Equipment
- Air & Gas Compressor Repair
- Art Schools
- Advertising & Promotional Gifts
- Animal Rights Organizations
- Adult Toys
- Agricultural Chemicals
- Awning & Canopy Cleaning
- Antique & Used Architectural Building Materials
- Animal Health
- Auto Racing Collectibles
- Aircraft
- Auto Glass
- Autographs & Manuscripts
- Airbrushing
- African Gift Shops
- Adult Foster Care
- Aluminum
- Auto Detailing Equipment
- Auto Electric Equipment
- Auto Diagnostic Equipment & Parts
- Apartment Information
- Airline Tickets

- Antique & Classic Auto Restoration & Repair
- Aircraft Painting & Livery Services
- Animal Registration & Identification Services
- Apartment Agencies
- Aptitude Testing
- Asbestos Training Services
- Air & Water Balancing Contractors
- Animal Hospitals
- Auto Starting Services
- Aviation Sports
- Advertising Signs
- Auto Air Conditioning & Heating
- Automation Equipment & Systems Industrial
- Aluminum Contractors
- Alcohol Testing Equipment
- Aerosols
- Acrylic
- Astrologers
- Antique & Classic Motorcycles
- Advertising & Promotional Mugs
- Acoustical Engineers
- Architectural Designers
- Agricultural Equipment
- Antique Coins
- Auto Service & Repair Consultants
- Auto Smog Devices
- Auto Diagnostic Equipment Repair
- Auctions
- Actuaries
- Answering & Finding Services
- Aromatherapy Skin Care
- Audio Books
- Air Pollution Controls & Systems
- Acupuncture Schools
- Audiovisual Production Services
- Antenna Master Systems
- Alzheimer's Care Facilities
- Architectural Metals
- Acupuncture Clinics
- Auto Emissions Testing
- Auto Gas Tanks Service
- Airline Support Services
- Auto Fleet Sales
- Auto Impounding Services
- Aerospace Support Services
- Advent Christian Churches
- Accident & Personal Injury Attorneys
- Aluminum Castings
- Audio Production & Recording
- Arbitrators
- Auto Insurance
- Artificial Flowers Supplies

- Advertising
  & Campaign Buttons
- Auto Mufflers
- Adult Chat
- Association Management
  Consultants
- Animal & Livestock
  Remedies
- Archery Instruction
- Auto Washing
  & Polishing Equipment
- ATM Locations
- Animal Assisted Therapy
- Auto Information
- Aircraft Parts
  & Equipment
- Aircraft Engines Service
- Airport Parking
- Allergy & Immunology
  Chiropractors
- Air Curtains & Screens
- Antique Rugs
- Aircraft Interiors
  & Upholstery
- Agricultural Storage
  Facilities
- Airport Transportation
- Animal Services
- Architectural Illustrators
- Aerospace Consultants
- Airports
- Attorneys
- Auto Trailer
- Asphalt Seal Coating
- Ambulance Services
- Aviation Consultants

- Animal Specialties
- Auto Racing Information
- Auto Recycling
  & Dismantling
- Automotive Engineers
- AIDS & HIV
  Information
- Audiovisual Consultants
- Abrasives & Abrasive
  Products
- Agricultural Aviation
  Seeding & Spraying
- Auto Appraisers
- Auto Oil & Lube
- Arthroscopy Orthopedics
  Surgeons
- Alcohol & Drug Abuse
  Information & Treatment
- Acupuncture
  Chiropractors
- Auto Bodies
- Auto Leasing
- Adult Trade Shows
  & Events
- Auto Buying Information
- Auto Body Repair
  & Painting
- Alliance Churches
- Adult Entertainers
- Armature Sales
  & Service
- Administrative
  Assistants Employment
  Agencies
- African Methodist
  Churches

- Auto Wrecking Equipment
- Arcade Games & Machines
- Armored Car Services
- Advertising Personnel Recruiters
- Allergy & Immunology Physicians & Surgeons
- Accounting & Tax Consultants
- Aquarium Maintenance Services
- Attendant Home Care Hospices
- Art Museums
- Aviation Schools
- Arbitration & Mediation Services Attorneys
- Agricultural Marketing
- Artificial Nails & Eyelashes
- Animal Breeders
- Architecture & Design Books
- Air Brushes
- Aluminum Fabricators
- Agricultural Loans
- Adult Videos & DVDs
- Air Sightseeing Tours
- Aircraft Charter
- Athletic Courts
- Alterations & Tailoring Equipment
- Antique Aircraft Restoration
- Advertising Specialties
- Antenna Towers
- Arcades & Amusements
- Agricultural Tractor Repair
- Accounting & Finance Software
- Adolescent Counselors
- Accounting & Bookkeeping Services
- Air Transportation
- Adjustable Beds
- Adult & Continuing Education
- Aircraft Transport
- Academic Specialty Schools
- Advertising Agencies
- Auto Wheel Covers & Hubcaps
- Antique Art Nouveau & Art Deco
- Antique Silver & Silverware
- Agricultural Services
- Alarm Services
- Allergy Equipment
- Art Classes
- Appraisers
- Adult Galleries
- Advertising Distribution Services
- Automated Fuel Services
- Air Couriers
- Asset Management
- Artists' Managers & Agents

- Architects
- Air Conditioning Consultants
- Agricultural Law Attorneys
- Air Ambulance Services
- Aromatherapy Products & Services
- Air Fresheners
- Aircraft Modification & Overhaul
- Adult Books
- Attic & Basement Finishing
- Airlines
- Activated Carbon
- Antique Repair & Restoration
- Art Supplies
- Antique & Classic Auto Parts
- Advertising & Design Agencies
- Auto Clutch Repair
- Antiques
- Auditors
- Avionics Sales & Service
- Animal Trapping Equipment
- Aircraft Appraisers
- Auto & Truck Lifts
- Air Cargo Services
- Automation Consultants
- Auto Engines Service & Repair
- Art Goods Moving & Storage
- Aluminum, Brass, Bronze & Magnesium Foundries
- Audiovisual Equipment Repair
- Air Conditioning Contractors' Equipment
- Adoption Attorneys
- Auto Performance & Racing Equipment
- AIDS & HIV Support Groups
- Air Conditioning Service
- Academic Caps & Gowns
- Apartment Buildings
- Air Conditioning Parts
- Agricultural Organizations
- Acupuncture & Acupressure
- Arts Organizations & Information
- Abortion Alternatives Information & Services
- Auto Consultants
- Adhesives & Glues
- Auto Interiors Repair & Refrigeration Compressors
- Aerospace
- Art & Jewelry Appraisers
- Alternative Fuels

- Advertising
  & Promotional Balloons
- Automated Answering
  Equipment & Systems
- Advertising &
  Promotional Awards
- Auto Damage Appraisers
- Allergy & Immunology
  Pediatrics Physicians
- Auto Machine Shop
  Services
- Aerial Surveyors
- Aircraft Support
  Equipment
- Animal Trappers
- Attorneys' Information
- Administrative
  & Governmental Law
  Attorneys
- Auto Tune Ups
- Analytical Chemists
- American Restaurants
- Architectural Services
- Auto Machine Shop
  Equipment
- Athletic Trainers
- Auto Differentials
- Agricultural Tractor
- Arbors & Trellises
- Accounting &
  Bookkeeping Schools
- Alcoholics Anonymous
- ASID Interior Decorators
  & Designers
- Air Quality Consultants
- Aquaculture
- Aircraft Cleaning

- Airport Equipment
- Auto Transport
- Aerospace Engineers
- Advertising Art Layout
  & Production Services
- Alternative Medicine
  Schools
- Antique
- Annuities
- Art Restoration
  & Conservation
- Aircraft Flight Training
  Equipment
- ATMs
- Animation Products
  & Services
- Auto Hand & Foot
  Controls
- Auto Mechanic Schools
- Alarm Systems
  Wholesale
- Air Conditioning
  Equipment Refrigerant
  Recovery
- Adventist Churches
- Art & Sculpture Books
- Aquatic Plants
- Auto Locks & Lockout
  Services
- Auto Tire Shop
  Equipment
- Antique Furniture
  & Lighting
- Accountants Information
- Art Paintings
- Accounting &
  Bookkeeping Machines

- Auto Alarms & Security Systems
- Air Motor
- Anodizing
- Asphalt Paving Contractors
- AIDS & HIV Physicians
- Adhesive & Glues
- Architects' Supplies
- Auctioneers & Auction Houses
- Advertising Directory & Guide Publishers
- Apostolic Churches
- Audio & Video Stores

B

- Boutiques
- Business Services
- Bridal Lingerie
- Beaches
- Business Answering Services
- Burial Caskets
- Beauty Salon Equipment
- Bottles
- Baby Accessories
- Barge Cleaning
- Biblical Counseling
- Bagels Wholesale
- Bed Springs
- Burglar Alarm Systems & Monitoring
- Burglar Alarms Installation, Service, & Repair

- Banking & Investment Law Attorneys
- Bar Code Scanning Equipment
- Building & House Moving Consultants
- Breastfeeding Information
- Building & Construction Trade Schools
- Business Insurance
- Battery Supplies
- Beds
- Body Art & Piercing
- Beauty Salon Equipment Service & Repair
- Barge & Tugboat
- Bulletproof Glass
- Band Instruments
- Boat Performance & Racing Equipment
- Boiler Heating - Residential
- Barbecue Restaurants
- Body Wrap Salons
- Backpacks & Handbags
- Bill Payment Services
- Business Management Services
- Bedroom Furniture
- Bank Auditing
- Bathroom Fixtures & Accessories
- Bins
- Business Books
- Business Accountants

- Bronze & Bronze Products
- Business Writers
- Bamboo, Rattan, & Wicker Home Furnishings
- Books & Magazines Wholesale & Distribution
- Burial Vaults
- Baseball Instruction
- Bridal Wear
- Bridal Supplies
- Boat Cushions
- Basement & Crawlspace Waterproofing
- Bicycle Repair & Maintenance
- Breast Pumps Sales
- Babysitting
- Bicycle Racks & Security Systems
- Bamboo Products
- & Furnishings
- Bail Bonds
- Business Valuators
- Blindness Residential Care
- Buttons & Badges
- Broadcasting Equipment
- Bed & Breakfast Reservations
- Bras & Girdles
- Boat Builders & Wholesalers
- Bowling Instruction
- Bakery Consultants
- Bronze Castings
- Boiler Tubes
- Blind Services & Facilities
- Birthing Centers
- Business Information
- Boring Contractors
- Bicycle Helmets
- Brass & Brass Product
- Bonsai Plants
- Brick
- Balloon Decorations
- Breweries
- Brushes & Brooms
- Bars & Pubs
- Billiards
- Boys' & Girls' Scouts' Uniforms
- Beauty Supplies
- Brakes Service & Repair
- Business Centers
- Bells & Chimes
- Business Form & Card Printing
- Blood Typing & Testing
- Bulk Oil
- Blinds
- Business to Business Direct Marketing
- Business Records Storage & Management
- Brush Removal Services
- Basketball Equipment
- Beach & Pool Cabanas
- Broken Glass

- Background & Foreground Music & Messages
- Brick Pavers
- Bathroom Accessories
- Boat Cleaning
- Bronze Tablets
- Building Code & Zoning Consultants
- Billiard Instruction
- Boiler Cleaning & Repair
- Bar Equipment Fixtures
- Bird Watching Services
- Bags
- Beauty & Day Spas
- Barber & Beauty Schools
- Brakes & Brake Parts
- Bird Supplies
- Barbecue Pits
- Batting Ranges
- Beekeepers
- Building Maintenance
- Beverages
- Builders' Hardware
- British Restaurants
- Bath Soaps
- Boat Houses, Lifts, & Hoists
- Business Development
- Back Supports
- Billing Services
- Bariatric Medicine Physicians & Surgeons
- Business Motivational Training
- Broadcasting Companies
- Bookcases & Bookstands
- Base Metals
- Badges
- Blueprinting Equipment Service & Repair
- Barges & Barge Lines
- Bakeries
- Bridal Shops
- Basement Repair & Restoration
- Balancing Service & Equipment Industrial
- Bible Churches
- Beer & Ale
- Business Cards
- Bricklayers
- Boat & Yacht Customizing
- Batteries
- Blood Banks
- Behavioral Medicine Pediatrics Physicians & Surgeons
- Bus Tours
- Brass Engravers
- Beauty Pageant Consultants
- Behavioral Medicine Psychiatrists & Psychologists
- Balloons
- Bulk Fuel Delivery
- Bakers' Equipment
- Bush Hogging
- Biofeedback Therapists

- Bird Barriers
  & Repellents
- Barbecues & Grills
  Service
- Burglar Alarm Response
  Services
- Business & Professional
  Associations
- Building/House Moving
  & Raising
- Bookbinders' Equipment
- Basketball Clubs
  & Instruction
- Beekeepers' Supplies
- Baptist Churches
- Baby Products
  & Accessories
- Breads
- Bulkheads
- Beverage Dispensing
  Equipment, Supplies,
  & Repair
- Barn Equipment
- Beauty Supplies
  & Equipment
- Basque Restaurants
- Beer Gardens
- Boxing Clubs
  & Instruction
- Boxes & Bags
- Birth Control & Family
  Planning Information
- Business Opportunities
- Beveled, Carved, &
  Etched Glass
- Business Audit
  Assistance

- Boat Covers, Tops,
  & Upholstery
- Bedding
- Backhoe & Bulldozer
  Service
- Bookstores
- Bushings
- Barricades
- Buy Here Pay Here Auto
- Bird Food
- Bicycle Trails
- Beer & Ale Distributors
- Bath Products
- Brick Paving Contractors
- Birds
- Builders & Contractors
- Beer Line Cleaning
  & Repair
- Building Contractors'
- Ballrooms
- Brazing
- Bagel Shops
- Blueprinting Equipment
- Boating Instruction
- Bus
- Biotechnology Products
- Bamboo
- Brewer Equipment
  Supplies
- Butchers
- Bedding Supplies
- Beads
- Bar Coding Services
- Baked Goods
- Business Computer
- Bicycle Parts

- Bathroom & Kitchen Contractors
- Bus Travel
- Bar Stools
- Boarding Stables
- Bird Hospitals
- Bonded Warehouses
- Battery Back Up Systems
- Ballroom & Social Dance Instruction
- Book Publishers
- Brass & Brass Products
- Bearings
- Baseball Clubs & Parks
- Boat Windows
- Bar Associations
- Business Multimedia Services
- Boots & Safety Shoes
- Blowers & Blowing Systems
- Burglar Bars & Resistant Equipment
- Butchers' Equipment
- Brazilian Restaurants
- Benches & Work Tables
- Business & Personal Coaching
- Boat Covers
- Bakery Restaurants
- Baton Twirling Instruction
- Banks
- Business & Professional Clubs
- Bottlers Equipment
- Beauticians
- Boat
- Belts & Suspenders
- Billiards Equipment
- Bottle
- Balsa Wood
- Bridges Contractors
- Binoculars & Telescopes
- Bookbinding
- Battery Charging Equipment Repair
- Bowling Equipment Service
- Beauty Salons
- Baskets
- Billiard Table Service
- Box Lunches
- Bowling Lane Refinishing
- Bulk Mail Processing
- Bookkeeping Services
- Bulletin & Directory Boards
- Batteries Industrial
- Barcode Labels
- Business Financing
- Brushes
- Boating & Marine Books
- Barbecue Equipment
- Buses
- Bomb Disposal Services
- Biological Products
- Barbecue Equipment
- Ballet Companies
- Bridal & Evening Shoes

- Barrels & Drums
- Bird Feeders & Houses
- Boilers
- Building Construction & Design Consultants
- Bowling Equipment
- Boat & Boat Trailer Storage
- Battery Rebuilding, Repairing, & Recharging
- Bridal Headpieces & Veils
- Boat Trailers
- Broadband Services
- Biological Laboratories
- Baseball Equipment
- Bus Tickets
- Brakes & Brake Linings
- Bed Bug Control & Removal Services
- Beach Accessories
- Business Colleges
- Burial Insurance
- Bark
- Blinds Installation, Cleaning, & Repair
- Bank Architects
- Buffet Restaurants
- Biofeedback Equipment
- Bottlers
- Brake Service Equipment
- Boudoir & Pin-Up Photography
- Bereavement Services
- Bistros
- Bathtubs & Sinks Repair
- Bumper Stickers
- Boat Licensing & Registration
- Buyers Information Services
- Bar & Grill Restaurants
- Bridal Gown
- Building & House Moving Machinery & Equipment
- Box Manufacturers Equipment
- Board Up Services
- Blind Organizations
- Barter Services
- Billiards Tables
- Bottled & Bulk Liquefied Petroleum Gas Equipment
- Bankruptcy Services
- Buttons
- Boat Restoration
- Boards of Education
- Bicycle Tours
- Bus Parts
- Bird Cages & Toys
- Blankets
- Biofeedback Equipment Service & Repair
- Bank Equipment
- Bathtubs
- Boat Insurance
- Baby Strollers
- Beef Jerky
- Boat Transport

- Brick Walkways & Patios
- Building Permits
- Boat & Yacht
- Broadcasting Schools
- Bartending Services
- Beauty Supplies & Equipment Repair
- Business Software
- Bowling
- Barbecued Meats
- Baby Furniture
- Bed
- Better Business Bureaus
- Blasting Contractors
- Bottle Caps & Seals
- Backhoes
- Buses Service & Repair
- Book & Manual Printing
- Bail Bond Companies
- Business Enterprises
- Barns
- Bedspreads
- Bus Charter
- Baby Products & Services
- Biomedical Engineers
- Basement Pumping Contractors
- Boat Painting & Refinishing
- Business Forms & Systems
- Breakfast & Brunch Restaurants
- Burger Restaurants
- Banquet Facilities
- Boxes
- Bowling Clothing
- Building Inspections Engineers
- Boat Repair
- Brethren Churches
- Beverage Coolers
- Boat Appraisers
- Building Materials
- Boat & Yacht Charters
- Bank Interiors Designers
- Bankruptcy Attorneys
- Bodyguard Services
- Barbers
- Boat Interiors
- Bath Scales
- Box Partitions
- Berean Churches
- Boat Hauling
- Bike Shops
- Boat Building Materials
- Boys' Clothing
- Bible Schools & Study
- Backflow Device Installation, Testing, & Service
- Book & Catalog Covers
- Boiler Equipment Industrial
- Braids & Tassels
- Beef Cattle
- Bleaching Compounds
- Birth Announcements
- Business Directory Publishers

- Building Construction Control Services
- Boiler Parts Manufacturers
- Billiard Table Recovering & Restoring
- Boiler Removal
- Beauty Consultants
- Building & House Leveling
- Business Interruption Insurance
- Bowling Alleys
- Big Screen Televisions
- Bartending Schools
- Building Restoration & Preservation
- Bathroom Remodeling
- Bottled & Bulk Water
- Ballet Schools
- Banquet Services
- Boiler Inspection
- Breakfast Nooks & Booths
- Bed & Breakfasts
- Building Remodeling & Repair Contractors'
- Beach & Cabana Clubs
- Breast Disease Physicians
- Business Cell Phone Equipment
- Basement Window Well Covers
- Booking Agents
- Botanical Gardens
- Battery Charging & Monitoring Equipment
- Bicycle Riding Instruction
- Bibles & Religious Books
- Business Planning Consulting Services
- Bicycles
- Beverage Bars
- Birth Records
- Bee Control & Removal Services
- Boat Trailers
- Bingo
- Blueprinting
- Baby Furniture
- Business Education
- Building Remodeling & Repair Contractors
- Balloons & Delivery
- Birthday Parties
- Buildings
- Bleachers & Grandstands Construction
- Breath Fresheners
- Back Care Products
- Bead Stringing
- Business Consultants
- Burglar Alarms
- Bowling Pro Shops
- Blacksmiths
- Baling Equipment
- Billiard Table Manufacturers

- Banners, Pennants, & Flags
- Barbers' Equipment
- Building & Home Construction
- Bakers' Equipment, Supplies, & Service
- Base Metal Refiners & Smelters

C

- China, Crystal, & Glassware
- Concrete Removal
- California Cuisine Restaurants
- Custom Maps
- Concrete Aggregates
- Computers & Equipment Installation
- Clock Moving Services
- Customs
- Chemical Spraying Services
- Carpenters
- Crafts & Craft Supplies
- Commuter & Public Transportation
- Communications Towers
- Cardiology Veterinarians
- Community Services Information & Referral
- Circus Schools
- Child Abuse Law Attorneys
- Calligraphers
- Computers & Electronics Recycling
- Credit Card Equipment
- Crime Prevention Programs
- Coins & Stamps
- Clothing Hangers
- Cheese
- Constitutional Law Attorneys
- Chocolate & Cocoa
- Cutlery
- Coin Operated Washing Machines & Dryers
- Ceramic Studios, & Equipment
- Catalog & Brochure Designers & Compilers
- Contract Packaging
- Chimney Lining Materials
- Canoe & Kayak
- Credit Cards
- Childbirth Education Consultants
- Churches Insurance
- Carpet Pads & Accessories
- Computer Systems Consultants & Designers
- Child Development Centers
- Ceramic Products Industrial
- Computer Disaster Recovery
- Custom Auto Painting

20

- Cemeteries & Crematories
- Catering Information Services
- Commercial Air Conditioning Equipment & Systems
- Car Pools & Ride Shares
- Chimneys
- Commercial & Industrial Appliance Sales & Repair
- Chrome Plating
- Credit & Debt Counseling Services
- Corporate Advertising Specialties & Promotions
- Construction Machinery & Equipment
- Commercial Laser Printing
- Cell Phone Equipment
- College Board Preparation Schools
- Chemicals
- Construction Trusses
- Computer Furniture
- Car Audio & Video Installation & Repair
- Copper & Copper Products
- Corporate Gifts
- Contraceptives
- Climbing, Hiking, & Backpacking
- Custom Printed T-Shirts
- Construction Consultants
- Contact Lens Consultants
- Casino & Gambling Equipment
- Cash Register
- Combustion & Heating Consultants
- China, Crystal, & Glassware Repair
- Concrete & Concrete Products
- Chicken Restaurants
- Commercial & Industrial Asphalt Paving Contractors
- Career & Workplace Education
- Child & Adolescent Guidance Counseling
- City Surveyors
- Construction Management
- Credit Investigators
- Children's Shoes
- Concession Stands
- Coupons
- Cold Storage Warehouses
- Computer Programming Instruction
- Concrete Products
- Construction Centers
- Crafts Instruction & Schools
- Carpet, Rug, & Upholstery Cleaning - Commercial & Industrial

- Cinder Blocks
- Copiers
- Cell Phone Service
- Clinics & Medical Centers
- Cosmetics
- Clean Rooms Equipment & Installation
- Computer Time Sharing Services
- Credit & Debt Services
- China & Glassware
- Common & Face Brick
- Collectible Gifts
- Chlorinators
- Crutches
- Cable, Conduit, & Poles Contractors
- Convention Security Consultants & Services
- Condominiums & Timeshares
- Credit Unions
- Credit Card Terminal Systems
- Cases
- Commercial & Industrial Bags
- Canoeing & Kayaking
- Convention Delivery Services
- Calculators & Adding Machines
- Coal & Coke
- Central Vacuum Cleaning Systems
- Corrugated & Fiber Boxes
- Consulates
- Children's Play Groups & Classes
- Countertops & Sink Tops
- Coats
- Cryogenics
- Computer Engineers
- Collectible Phonograph Records
- Construction Control Services
- Citrus Fruits
- Condiments & Sauces
- Ceiling Fans
- Carpet & Rug Contractors
- Child Care Centers
- CDs, Tapes, & Records
- Church Supplies
- Clown Supplies
- Clothing Accessories
- Cash Registers
- Candy & Confectionery
- Computer Networks
- Cable Television Advertising
- Carpet Cleaning Equipment
- Chemical Toilets
- Credit Management Services
- Carnival Equipment
- Chemical Engineers
- Control Panels

- Cranes & Derricks Service
- Construction Quality Control
- Counseling Services
- Cleaning Compounds
- Children's & Infants' Clothing
- Computer Cable & Wire Installation
- China & Crystal
- Corporate Image Development Services
- Collectible Dolls
- Canoe Trip Outfitters
- Charismatic Churches
- Child Abuse Treatment Centers
- Construction Consulting & Management Services
- Cesspool Building & Service
- Ceramic Tiles
- Cookies & Crackers
- Catalog & Brochure Printing
- Concrete Pumping Service
- Consumer Electronics Stores
- Computer & Equipment
- Conservative Synagogues
- Commercial Printing
- Ceramic Arts
- Crisis Centers
- Corporate Insurance Adjusters
- Concrete Driveways & Sidewalks
- Clothing Storage
- Color Consultants
- Cafes
- Clairvoyants
- Computers Executive Search Firms
- Custom Shirts
- Class Rings & Pins
- Commercial Vehicle
- Chiropractic Clinics
- Chimney Building & Repair - Commercial
- Condominiums & Townhomes
- Commercial & Industrial Architects
- Corporate Housing
- Classrooms
- Clothing & Accessories Consignment & Resale
- Canvas Goods Repair
- Credit Card Protection Services
- Custom Printed Shirts
- Concrete Contractors - Commercial & Industrial
- Cake Decorating Services
- Collating Equipment
- Christian Churches
- Cremation Urns
- Container Services

- Concrete Breaking, Coring, Cutting, & Sawing Equipment
- Commercial & Industrial Appraisers
- Convention Translators & Interpreters
- Calvary Chapel Churches
- Cruise Lines & Agents
- Country Dining Restaurants
- Certified Public Accountants
- Cake & Pie Shops
- Commercial Tractors
- Cabinets & Cabinet Makers - Commercial & Industrial
- Counseling Centers
- Coffee Roasting & Equipment
- Choreographers
- Children's Books
- Children Photographers
- Cemeteries Equipment
- Concrete Repair & Restoration Contractors
- Cold Storage Equipment
- Custom Car Parts
- Concrete Additives
- Carpet & Furniture Stain Protection
- Computer Graphics & Imaging
- Community Homes
- Consumer Protection Attorneys
- Charitable & Nonprofit Organizations
- Cafeterias
- Casino Equipment
- Comedy Clubs
- Cardiac Rehabilitation Centers
- Collectible Guns
- Convenience Store Delicatessens
- Concrete Construction Equipment
- Craniosacral Therapy
- Crane
- Contractors' Traffic Control Signs
- Computer Graphics Equipment
- Custom Kitchen Cabinets
- Cable Television Services
- Computer Parts
- Cable Assemblies
- Contractors' Signs
- Comforter & Mattress Covers & Pads
- Community Services
- Communications & Electronic Contractors
- Campers
- Canning Equipment
- Crane & Derrick
- Clergy & Pastoral Counselors

- Christmas Decorating
- Computer Supplies, & Parts
- Collision Services
- Concrete Mixers
- Caulking Contractors
- Chemicals - Commercial & Industrial
- Closed Circuit Television Equipment & Security Systems
- Cruises Travel Agents
- Coffee & Tea
- Contractors Tools & Fasteners
- Convention & Meeting Facilities & Services
- Commercial & Industrial Building Materials
- Commercial & Graphic Artists
- Concrete & Pumice Brick
- Computer Animation
- Correctional Institutions
- Construction Trusses
- Compost
- Car Audio & Video
- Custom Made Carpets & Rugs
- Casters & Glides
- Credit Reporting Agencies
- Copying Consultants
- Custom Made Riding Clothes

- Carpet, Rug, & Upholstery Services
- Chemical Plant Equipment
- Consultants' Support Services
- Constables
- Concrete Ditch Liners
- Commercial Fishing
- Community Services Agencies
- Cork & Cork Products
- Child Care Consultants
- Cemetery Lots
- Court Transcribers
- Canvas Custom Products
- Computer Books
- Consumer Organizations & Cooperatives
- Cameras & Camera Supplies
- Camcorders
- Chemists
- Catholic Churches
- Check Protection Equipment
- Cabinet Making Supplies
- Computer Cleaning
- Commercial Building Inspection
- Clay & Clay Products
- Ceiling Materials
- Cell Phones
- Communications Equipment Manufacturers

- Concrete Breaking, Coring, Cutting, Drilling, & Sawing
- Commercial & Savings Banks
- Computer Music Products
- Computer Service Bureaus
- Convention & Visitors Photographers
- Chiropractors
- Circuit Board Assembly
- Commercial & Industrial Awnings & Canopies
- CPAP Equipment
- Carpet, Rug, & Upholstery Cleaning
- Clinical Psychologists
- Commercial Air Duct Cleaning
- Carpenters - Commercial
- Convention Party Planning
- Concrete Buildings
- Chess Equipment
- Cabinet Refacing, Refinishing, & Resurfacing
- Check Signing & Endorsing Machines
- Contractors' Materials Handling Equipment
- Childbirth Education
- Convention & Meeting Planning Services
- Cremation Services
- Cocktail Mixes
- Career & Vocational Counseling
- Carcass Removal Services
- Church of Christ Churches
- Cosmetic & Reconstructive Surgeons
- Courier & Delivery Services
- Corn & Corn Cob Products
- Cargo Trailer
- Crushing, Pulverizing, & Shredding Equipment
- Computer Systems Integration
- Carpet & Rug Installation Equipment
- Closets & Closet Accessories
- Collectible & Vintage Clothing
- Corporate Limousine Services
- County Clerk
- Cancer Information & Treatment Services
- Crates & Crating Industrial
- Christmas Decorations & Lights
- Containerized Freight Trucking
- Contamination Control Services

- Ceiling Contractors
- Cat
- College Preparatory Schools
- Consumer Information
- Children's Furniture
- Cooling Towers
- Convention Exhibits & Displays
- Chillers
- Custody & Support Law Attorneys
- Child Abuse Hotline
- Cleaning Compounds
- Counter Tops
- Concessionaires Equipment
- Colleges & Universities
- Coal Miners & Shippers
- Corporate Gift Baskets
- Costumers & Designers
- Climbing Gyms
- Children's & Infants' Accessories
- Cash Advance Loans
- Charitable & Nonprofit Fundraising
- Cast Stone
- Chairs
- Crime Victim Services
- Custom Wedding Dresses
- Construction Heaters
- Couplings
- Cartoon & Caricature Artists
- Cargo Insurance
- Convenience Stores
- Camping Equipment
- Cell Phone
- Concrete Curing & Treating Materials
- Children's Transportation Services
- Carpets & Rugs - Commercial & Industrial
- Crystals
- Custom Cabinets
- Carpet Consultants
- Community & Civic Organizations
- Compressor
- Child & Adolescent Psychiatry Physicians
- Clothing Printing & Lettering
- Color Copying Services
- Clams
- Corrosion Prevention Engineers
- Charcoal
- Cookware & Cooking Utensils
- Caregivers
- Cameras Service & Repair
- Carpets & Rugs
- Clothing Consultants
- Computer Software
- Carpet & Rug Weavers
- Concrete Pipe

- Christian Science Churches
- Conveyors & Conveying Equipment
- Clerical Employment Agencies
- Carburetors
- Coastal Engineers
- Custom Steel Fabricators
- Cactus
- Crushing & Pulverizing Service
- Carpet & Rug Materials
- Commercial & Graphic Arts
- Culverts
- Carbon Products
- Computer Marketing Employment Agencies
- Carpet Workrooms
- Christian Ministries
- Clambake Caterers
- Courier & Delivery Services - Residential
- Cigar & Cigarette Accessories
- Cake & Candy Decorating Equipment
- Continental Cuisine Restaurants
- Candles
- Consumer Audiovisual Equipment
- Computer Storage Devices Manufacturers
- Certified General Accountants
- Coffee
- Computer Security Systems
- Cardiology Pediatrics Physicians & Surgeons
- Communications Equipment
- Child Care Services
- Construction Surveyors
- Christian Schools
- Cake & Candy Making Equipment
- Cosmetic & Reconstructive Pediatrics Surgeons
- Cranes & Derricks Parts & Accessories
- Children's Sports Programs
- Career Planning & Employment Assistance Services
- Cooking Services
- Christian Science Reading Rooms
- CD & Cassette Tape Duplication Services
- Contemporary Art Galleries
- Construction Engineers
- Call Centers
- Cantonese Restaurants
- Cylinders Rebuilding & Repairing
- Chapels
- Campgrounds & RV Parks

- Copyright & Trademark Services
- Ceramic Products
- Certified Midwives
- Chauffeurs
- Cable Television Equipment
- Computer Terminal Manufacturers
- Cat Breeders
- Computer Programmers Employment Agencies
- Cotton & Cotton Goods
- Child Care Information
- Cemeteries & Memorial Parks
- Ceramic Tile Installation & Repair
- Construction Materials
- Climate Controlled Storage
- Contact Lenses
- Cabinets & Cabinet Making Supplies
- Carpet & Upholstery Cleaning Equipment
- Commercial & Industrial Bottled & Bulk Water
- Civil Engineers
- Court Reporting Schools
- Child Support
- Clothing
- Cast Stone Manufacturers
- Church Retreats
- Convention & Trade Show Coordinators
- Core Drilling Contractors
- Condominium Office
- Concrete Construction Equipment
- Court Reporting
- Cedar & Cedar Products
- Children's Services Organizations
- Church of Jesus Christ of Latter Day Saints
- Columns
- Custom Hauling Services
- Convention Supplies
- Credit Rating Corrections Services
- Cosmetic Dentists
- County Government Offices
- Contractors' Equipment Service & Repair
- Car Leasing
- Custom Hydraulic Hoses & Fittings
- Concrete Curbing
- Costume Jewelry
- Commercial Laundries
- Canoe & Kayak
- Credit Card Merchant Services
- Computer Repair
- Ceramics Schools
- Card & Game Playing Rooms
- Computer Printers
- Collectibles

- Church Construction & Contractors
- CNC Machining, Turning & Milling Shops
- Carpet & Rug Binding Machines
- Creditors' Rights Attorneys
- Cultural Attractions, Events, Conventions & Facilities
- Construction Services
- Coil & Flat Springs
- Custom Woodworking
- Church Organs
- Cooperative Grocers
- Children's Parties
- Cat Hospitals
- Coffee Makers
- Copying & Duplicating Services
- Clutches & Facings
- Church of the Nazarene
- Collection Law Attorneys
- Cycling Clothes
- Cookbooks
- Carports
- Courts
- Computer Room Installation
- Closed Captioning Services
- Cistern Builders
- Concierge Services
- Car Storage
- Condominiums & Townhomes
- Cigar Storage Equipment
- Conferences & Conventions
- Collection Agencies
- Construction Estimators
- Commercial & Industrial Building Contractors
- Communication Technology Services
- Comic Books Bought & Sold
- Closet Systems & Organizers
- Colleges & Universities Information
- Cement
- Cupcake Shops
- Candle Holders
- Culinary Schools
- Congregational Churches
- Consumer Protection Services
- Cutting & Slitting Services
- Custom Jewelry
- Carpet & Rug Inspection & Measuring Services
- Chemical Analysis Laboratories
- Crowd Control Equipment
- Canoe & Kayak Trips
- Condominium & Townhouse Management

- Carpet, Rug, & Upholstery Dyers
- Chiropractic Information
- Clean Room Garments
- CPR Instruction
- Concrete Patching Compounds
- Concrete Blocks & Shapes - Commercial & Industrial
- Citizenship Instruction
- Clothing Stores
- Custom Clothing
- Commercial Bookbinders
- Christmas Shops
- Caterers - Commercial
- Carpet & Rug Installation
- Conventions, Trade Shows & Conferences
- Carbide Metals & Products
- Color Matching Service
- Colors & Pigments
- Charter Schools
- Chiropractic Equipment
- Charities
- Candles & Candle Equipment
- Cable Detection, Installation, & Splicing
- Carpet & Rug
- Contract Haulers
- Covenant Churches
- Coin Operated Car Wash & Polish
- Caterers
- Carbon Monoxide Testing
- Child Foster Care
- Commercial Shopping Services
- Church Financing
- Cellular PCS
- Cuban Restaurants
- Child Therapists
- Concrete Construction Forms & Accessories
- Contractors' Equipment
- Cooling Radiators
- Custom Designed Aquariums
- Coin Supplies Wholesale
- Ceramics Equipment
- Colonic Therapy
- Community Churches
- Commercial Loans
- Crab House Restaurants
- Child Safety Products
- Custom Home Builders
- Coin & Money Handling Equipment
- Construction Law Attorneys
- Cabinet Installation
- Copying & Duplicating Services - Commercial
- Commercial Air Conditioning Service & Repair
- Computer Enhancements

31

- Crushed & Broken Limestone
- Corporate Finance & Securities Attorneys
- Child Abuse Information
- Catering Equipment
- Cloth Bags
- Civic Clubs & Organizations
- Computers & Technology Law Attorneys
- Cleaning Equipment
- Commercial Paper
- Catch Basin Covers
- Cosmetic Tattoos
- Computer Technology Schools
- Catalogs & Brochures
- Cabinets
- Canoe & Kayak Equipment
- Cemetery & Memorial Park Maintenance
- Credit & Charge Plans
- Clean Room Facilities
- Custom Made Golf Clubs
- Concrete Grinding & Finishing
- Check Collection Services
- Central Vacuum Cleaning System
- Cajun & Creole Restaurants
- Clowns
- Convention Display Designers
- Construction Companies
- Composting Equipment
- Cash Registers Repair
- Christ's Church Churches
- Computer Room Monitoring & Management
- Card Access Control Systems
- Computer Network Hardware
- Cutting Tools
- Computer Networking Installation
- Courier & Delivery Services - Commercial & Industrial
- Clinical Social Workers
- Concrete Tanks
- Computer Technical Support Employment Agencies
- Computer Records Management
- Cocktail Lounges
- Cylinder Heads & Blocks Rebuilding & Repairing
- Creative Writers
- Chandeliers
- Control Systems & Regulators
- Custom Tile Design
- Construction Clean Up Contractors

- Corporate Gift Services
- Canvas Goods
  & Products
- Cancer Insurance
- Church of Jesus Christ
  Churches
- Check Verification
  Services
- Contractors' Information
- Coupon Redemption
- Compressed Natural Gas
- Carpet Sweepers
- Clock & Repair
- Concrete Reinforcements
- Clergy
- Concrete Coatings
- Cooling Systems
  Industrial
- Carnivals, Fairs,
  & Festivals
- Closet Accessories
- Camps
- Concrete Sealing
  & Waterproofing
- Corrugated Metals
- Coffee Maker Repair
- Chinese Restaurants
- Commercial Auto Bodies
- Concrete Post
  Tensioning Contractors
- Closets & Closet
  Accessories-Commercial
- Camping & Travel
  Trailer
- Concert Bureaus
- Commercial Auto

- Chicago Style
  Restaurants
- Coffee Mills
- Carbon Dioxide
- Chambers of Commerce
- Caribbean Restaurants
- Cigar, Cigarette,
  & Tobacco
- Computer Aided Design
  Services
- Commercial Air
  Conditioning Contractors
- Chiropractic X-Ray
  Laboratories
- Community Centers
- Calibration & Gauge
  Testing Laboratories
- Computer Hardware
- Criminal Law Attorneys
- Check Cashing Services
- Crabs & Crab Products
- Crisis Intervention
  Services
- Construction Site
  Development
  Contractors
- Candy & Cookie
  Arrangements
- Colon & Rectal Surgeons
- Clothing & Accessories
- Compound Plastics
  Manufacturers
- Custom Corrugated
  Boxes
- Cleaning Services
- Computers & Equipment

- Chemical Clean-Up & Control Services
- Classified Advertising
- Chefs
- Camping & Travel Trailers Service & Repair
- Customer Service Representatives
- Corral Builders
- Casinos
- Custom Printed Jackets
- Commercial Signs
- Contractors Tractors
- Crushed Stone
- Consulting Engineers
- Convention & Trade Show Promotion
- Check Processing Services
- Clothing Labels
- Chain Saw Sales & Service
- Chains
- Crankshaft Grinding
- Crime & Trauma Scene Cleaning Services
- Children's Nursing & Rehabilitation Centers
- Court Bailiffs
- Chinese Foods
- Communications & Public Relations Consultants
- Custom Embroidered Sportswear

- Children's & Infants' Gifts
- Church Camps
- Clinics
- Credit Card Plans & Services
- Cranes, Hoisting, & Rigging Services
- Concrete Mixers
- Custom Shoes & Boots
- Computer & Software Technical Support
- Casino Transportation Services
- Copyright Services
- Construction Information Services
- Conveyor Belting & Belting Supplies
- Consignment Services & Shops
- Certified & Registered Massage Therapists
- Copiers
- Cushions
- Conference Call Services
- Church Furnishings
- Continuous & Individual Forms Printing
- Circuses
- Cheese Shops
- Check Printing
- Church of God in Christ
- Custom Photofinishing

- Cell Phone Repair & Installation
- Coffee Break Service
- College Consultants
- Chimney Cleaning Equipment
- Coupon & Ticket Printing
- Cabinets & Cabinet Makers - Residential
- Cigar Bars
- Closet Design & Remodeling
- Concert Tickets
- Churches
- Communications Services
- Composting Facilities
- Coal Mining Services
- Chimney Tops & Caps
- Cheerleading & Instruction
- Cables & Wires
- Communications Engineers
- Chemical Water Purification
- Cigars & Cigarettes Mail Order
- Carpet & Rug Cleaners Information
- Cutting Oils
- Church Support Services
- Cardiology Physicians
- Costumes
- Child Care Center Consultants
- Cell Phone
- Comforters
- Cut Stone & Stone Products Manufacturers
- Christ Centered Churches
- Court & Convention Reporters
- Cars Service & Repair
- Corporate Business Attorneys
- Crude Oil
- Cancer Clinics
- Credit Insurance
- Circuit Breakers
- Convention Exhibit & Display
- Credit Restoration
- Crane Inspection & Testing
- Custom Lamp Shades
- Church of God Churches
- Carbide Tools
- Christian Counselors
- Chiropractic Schools
- Ceramic Tile Contractors
- Calendars, Planners, & Organizers
- Charitable, Educational, & Research Foundations
- Cabin, Cottage, & Chalet
- Coupon Services
- Casino & Gaming Equipment
- Civil Law Attorneys
- Catholic Schools

- College & University Online Courses
- Canvas
- Commodity & Merchandise Warehouses
- Christmas Trees & Wreaths
- Clocks
- Computer Upgrade Services
- Child Care Agencies
- Copywriters
- Chemical Storage & Handling
- Concrete Blocks & Shapes
- Condominiums Maintenance
- Computer Telephony
- Chicken Take Out
- Commercial Auto Air Conditioning
- College & University Placement Services
- Children's Furniture Stores
- Chimney Cleaning Services
- Country Clubs
- Comic Books
- Costume Sales
- Computer Training
- Chlorine & Chlorinated Products
- Computer & Software Stores
- Contemporary & Modern Furniture Stores
- Cabinet Hardware
- Concrete Contractors
- Computer & Electronics Movers
- Concrete Floor Coating
- Commercial & Industrial Auctioneers
- Crushed Rock
- Colombian Restaurants
- Convention Visitors
- & Information Centers
- Credit Card Verification Equipment Sales & Services
- Coffee & Tea Shops
- College Financial Planning Services
- Copiers Service & Repair
- Cigars, Cigarettes, & Tobacco
- Coral
- Computer Consultants
- Catfish Restaurants
- Children's & Family Entertainment
- Computer Peripherals
- Color Printing
- Custom Leather Goods
- Conveyor & Monorail Systems

<u>D</u>

- Dermatology Physicians
- Door & Window
- Delicatessens
- Divorce Services
- Draperies & Curtains
- Diamond Cutters
- Directory & Guide Publishers
- Document Examiners
- Design
- Dermatology Podiatry Physicians & Surgeons
- Data Recovery
- Diesel Fuel Injection Service, Sales, & Parts
- Door & Window Screen Sales & Repair
- Department Stores
- Drive Shafts
- Deliverance Churches
- Dollar Stores
- Dressmakers
- Dishwasher Sales & Service
- Data Processing Services Computer Outsourcing
- Diabetes Physicians
- Data Storage
- Distilled Water
- Drapery & Curtain Fabrics
- Dishwashers - Commercial
- Door & Door Frame
- Dry Cell Batteries

- Designer Clothing
- Dude Ranches
- Doll Houses & Accessories
- Deck Designers & Builders
- Duct & Duct Fittings
- Dune Buggies
- Drapery & Curtain Cleaning Services
- Dock Covers & Seals
- Dyes & Dyestuffs
- Diamonds
- Drafting Engineers
- Dress Trimmings
- Diesel Engines
- Data Communications Service & Repair
- Domestic Aprons
- Disappearing Beds
- Dry Ice
- Divorce Counseling & Mediation
- Diagnostic Imaging Chiropractors
- Developmentally Disabled Homes
- Distilled Water Wholesale
- Dentures
- Developmental Disabilities
- Draperies & Custom Curtains
- Disability Law Attorneys
- DJ Equipment

- Dog Houses
- Drain Services
- Drug Charges Attorneys
- Drafting Equipment
- Drilling Contractors
- Dried Fruits
- Dormer Construction
- Dermatology Veterinarians
- Door Closers & Checks Repair
- Drywall Equipment
- Dictating Machines
- Drain Pipes & Tiles
- Dressmakers' Wedding Services
- Digital Phones
- Diving Tours
- Diners
- Digital Printers
- Divorce Attorneys
- Drilling & Boring Machines
- DSL Services
- Dining Furniture
- Drawing Materials
- Diving Equipment
- Door & Gate Operating Devices Repair
- Discing Services
- Diesel Oils
- Doulas
- Disability Employment Agencies
- Deck Materials
- Dial A Ride Services
- Dock Hardware
- Drapery & Curtain Alterations
- Dental Insurance
- Debt Adjusters
- Diesel Generators
- Door Closers & Checks
- Dental Hygienists
- Deck Cleaning & Treatment
- Dry Docks
- Dental Public Health
- Dance Clothing
- Dredging Machinery
- Dental Practice Management
- Drafting Employment Agencies
- Data Communications Equipment & Systems
- Driveway Coating Materials
- Discount Stores
- Driver Testing
- Display Designers & Producers
- Decorative Glass
- Domestic Violence Counseling
- Deck Construction & Maintenance
- Domestic Partnerships Attorneys
- Dental Laboratories
- Digital Imaging Equipment

- Data Processing Consultants
- Document Management Services
- Dry Cleaners Equipment
- Drilling Chucks
- Dance Companies
- Disability Services
- Dry Cleaners Equipment Service & Repair
- Dog Enclosures & Runways
- Dispensing Opticians
- Diapers & Diaper Services
- Dry Cleaners Delivery Service
- Dewatering Contractors
- Data Storage Media
- Dry Cleaners
- Dolls & Accessories
- Designers
- Driveway Contractors & Construction
- Drainage Engineers
- Dehumidifying Equipment, Supplies, & Service
- Drapery Workrooms
- Design & Communications Agencies
- Dog & Cat Supplies
- Drivers' License Testing
- Directory & Guide Advertising
- Drafting Services
- Darts & Dartboards
- Door & Door Frame Hardware & Parts
- Drugs & Medications
- Database Management Software
- Data Processing Equipment
- Display & Exhibit Movers
- Defense Contractors
- Dental Equipment Repair
- DNA Testing
- Dialysis Clinics
- Die Cutting
- Door & Window Screens
- Doors & Door Frames - Commercial & Industrial
- Diving Instruction
- Desktop Publishing Printing
- Driving Schools
- Dental Equipment
- Data Communications Cabling
- Dietitians
- Digital Cameras
- Diabetes Associations
- Diabetic Services
- Desktop Publishing
- Digging & Hoisting Buckets
- Drywall Repair
- Down Bedding
- Dance Clubs

- Door & Window Screen Cleaning
- Dim Sum Restaurants
- Dental Technicians
- Data Conversion Services & Software
- Disability Accommodation Consultants
- Die Cut Printing
- Denture Service Centers
- Debt Consolidation
- Dorms
- Dairy Stores
- Diplomas & Certificates
- Debt Consolidation Attorneys
- Disabled & Handicapped Telecommunications Equipment
- Drums Instruction
- Dog Parks
- Dock Materials
- Dog Breeders
- Driving Information
- Dump Trucking
- Door Hanging & Installation
- Dating Services
- Dance Supplies
- Disc Jockeys
- Disinfectants
- Domestic Violence Information & Services
- Demolition Consultants
- Disabilities & Special Needs Equipment
- Davits
- Dairy Products
- Diamonds & Buyers
- Demolition - Residential
- Dog & Horse Racing
- Dust Collection Equipment
- Driveways - Residential
- Dental Phobia Dentists
- Disposable Products
- Decorative & Art Posters
- Decorative Metal Welding
- Dog Training
- Duplicating Machines
- Dishwasher Parts
- Deburring
- Dresses
- Dentists Organizations
- Dental Clinics
- Dating Services Information
- Direct Marketing & Sales
- Direct Mail Advertising
- Dolls
- Desks
- Dock boards & Ramps
- Diesel Fuel
- Dust Control Materials
- Dumbwaiters
- Dental Implants
- Door Repair
- Dental Schools

- Decorating Services
  - Residential
- Dentists
- Dredging Contractors
- Decals
- Demonstration Services
- Data Systems
  Consultants
- Drywall
- Dairy Equipment Repair
- Domestic Help
  Employment Agencies
- Direct Mail Printing
- Developmental Vision
  Optometrists
- Desserts
- Doll Clothes
- Drill Bits
- Dairy Bar Restaurants
- Dairy Farms
- Ditching Contractors
- Duct Work
- Dry Well Contractors
- Delivery & Errand
  Services
- Discount Furniture
  Stores
- Data Processing Schools
- DUI Schools
- Door & Window Guards
- Dentists Group &
  Corporate Practice
- Doors & Windows
  Installation
- Discrimination & Civil
  Rights Attorneys
- Diabetes Clinics
- Drapery & Curtain
  Fixtures
- Driver Training
  Equipment
- Dry Rot Repair
- Dirt Contractors
- Dry Mixed Concrete
- Dairy Equipment
- Directional Drilling
  Contractors
- Digital Imaging
- Door Glass
- Document Preparation
  Services
- Diamond Setters
- Docks
- Digital Imaging
  Photographers
- Diamonds Industrial
- Divorce Services
  Information
- Distribution Services
- Dental Laboratory
  Equipment
- Dessert Restaurants
- Dog & Cat Food
- Decorative & Specialty
  Concrete
- Defense Consulting
  Agencies
- Day Camps
- Dance Consultants
- Decorative Sea Shells
- Disciples of Christ
  Churches

- Dolls Repair & Restoration
- Display Equipment, Fixtures, & Materials
- Dehydrated & Freeze Dried Foods
- Developmental Disabilities Information & Services
- Dance Studios
- Deck Maintenance
- Denturists
- Door Glass & Mirrors
- Drug & Alcohol Detection & Testing
- Disabilities & Special Needs Clothing
- Dog Doors
- Drainage Contractors
- Dock Builders & Services
- Doors & Windows
- Disabled & Elderly Home Health Care
- Delicatessen Products
- Design & Build Contractors
- Decorative Shelving
- Die Cutting Equipment
- DVD Kiosks
- Dermatology Pediatrics Physicians & Surgeons
- DUI/DWI Attorneys
- Drainage Tile Contractors
- Doll Parts
- Doors & Door Frames
- Driveway & Parking Lot Blacktop Contractors
- Disc Golf
- Drilling & Boring Equipment
- Dance Halls
- Drain Odor Detection
- Detective Agencies
- Diamond Appraisers
- Diabetic Equipment
- Data Processing Services Postal Optimization
- Drapery & Curtain Trimmings
- Defensive Driving Instruction
- Dairy Consultants
- Data Processing Equipment Maintenance
- Dog Breeders Information
- Dental Information
- Data Processing Services Data Entry
- Decorative & Building Stone
- Driveway Sealing
- Domestic Violence Shelters
- Decorative Painting
- Dinner Theaters
- Donuts
- Debt Settlement
- Decorative Concrete Resurfacing Contractors
- Data Processing Services
- Drywall Contractors

- Dog Training Supplies
- Disability Insurance
- Dance Instructors
- Data Processing Employment Agencies
- Display Installation Services
- Dentistry Veterinarians
- Dress Gloves
- Dryer Vent Cleaning
- Dancers

E

- Emergency Notification Services
- Electric Converters
- Elements & Alloys
- Environmental Assessment Services
- Excavating & Ditching Equipment
- Electric Fuses
- Engineering Equipment
- Environmental Control Systems
- Equestrian Sports & Recreation
- Energy
- Electric Wire Harnesses
- Electronics Engineers
- Estate Planning & Administration
- Electric Motor Parts & Repair
- Exercise & Fitness Classes & Instruction

- Electric Equipment Service
- Ethiopian Restaurants
- Elevators - Residential
- Employment Agencies
- Escalators
- Electric Tools
- Energy Equipment, Systems,
- Employee Benefit & Compensation Plans
- Espresso Machines
- Eaves Troughs
- Explosives
- Electric Control Equipment
- Elevator Consultants
- Energy Engineers
- Extended Stay Hotels
- Engineering Surveys
- Export Representatives
- Electric Equipment Job Lots
- E-Commerce
- Elder Care
- Electronic & Fax Advertising
- Estate Planning & Administration Attorneys
- Ethnic Grocers
- Eating Disorders Information & Treatment Centers
- Educational Charitable & Nonprofit Organizations

- Executives Employment Agencies
- Emergency Disaster Restoration
- Electric Contractors - Commercial & Industrial
- Excavation Contractors
- Emergency Services Veterinarians
- Emergency Disaster Planning
- Escort Information
- Exotic & Luxury Car
- Embroidery & Needlework Supplies
- Emergency & Critical Care Physicians & Surgeons
- Exotic Birds
- Electronic Publishing
- Eminent Domain & Condemnation Attorneys
- Episcopal Churches
- Ear, Nose, & Throat Physicians & Surgeons
- Embroidering Machines
- Electric Panels & Switchboards
- Espresso
- Emergency Lighting Equipment
- Electric Companies
- Emergency & Critical Care Pediatrics Physicians
- Employment & Labor Law Attorneys
- Ear Piercing Equipment
- Emergency Power Systems
- Elevator Parts
- Electronic Banking Systems
- Educational Exhibits
- Emergency Ambulance Services
- Energy Marketing
- Electrical Designers
- Ethnic, Culture, & Language Books
- Export Consultants
- Engineers Employment Agencies
- Expert Testimony Services
- Environmental Products
- Education Law Attorneys
- Electronic Books
- Economic Research & Analysis
- Electronic Enclosures
- Electric Heating
- Electronic Power Supplies
- Elderly Companion Services
- Electric Contractors - Residential
- Embroidery Service
- Electric Signs
- Ethnic Jewelry

- Engines Rebuilding & Service
- Energy Conservation Products & Services
- Emergency Disaster Recovery
- Evangelical Churches
- Events Photographers
- Etched & Sandblasted Glass
- Electronic Components
- Energy & Environment
- Educational Consultants
- Energy Code Compliance Analysts
- Engineering Services
- Electric Tools - Commercial
- Earth Homes Builders
- Energy Management & Conservation Consultants
- Electrical Engineers
- Electric Instruments
- Emergency Medical Training
- Environmental & Natural Resources Attorneys
- Educational Financing
- Engineering Reports
- Euro Asian Restaurants
- Elementary & Secondary Education
- Employee Counseling Services
- Electro medical Equipment
- Electrolysis Equipment
- Electrical Inspection
- Erosion Control
- Ergonomics
- Essential Oils
- Employment Background Checks
- Electrostatic Painting
- Event Coordinators
- Environmental Health & Safety Services
- Electric Fixtures
- Embroidery & Needlework
- Employment Training Services
- Environmental Medicine Physicians & Surgeons
- Excess & Surplus Insurance
- Electric Conduit & Fittings
- Employment Opportunities
- Ecological Engineers
- Environmental Site Assessment & Remediation
- Educational Services
- Electric Heating Equipment
- Employment
- Election Law Attorneys
- Erotic Massage & Body Work

- Ergonomics Consultants
- Endocrinology & Metabolism Pediatrics Physicians
- Educational Equipment
- Entertainment & Sports Law Attorneys
- Electronic Transformers
- European Restaurants
- Embossing
- Electronic Component Manufacturers
- East Indian Restaurants
- Email Services
- Environmental Engineers
- Endocrinology & Metabolism Physicians & Surgeons
- Email Marketing
- Electromagnetic Measurements & Testing
- Embroidery
- Environmental Services Insurance
- Elevator Contractors
- Employment Placement Consultants
- Executive Coaching Consultants
- Educational Research
- Employee Benefit Administration
- Etiquette Schools
- Expansion Anchors
- Engineers
- Employment Preparation Services
- Electric Motor Controls
- Enrolled Agents
- Electronic Musical Instruments
- Envelopes
- Environmental Organizations
- Electric Equipment
- Emergency Preparedness
- Estate Appraisal & Liquidation
- Examination & Surgical Gloves
- Eggs
- Elevator Remodeling
- Energy Management Systems & Products
- Exhaust Systems
- Electric Connectors
- Exterior House & Building Washing
- Elevators & Escalators
- Environmental Training
- Entertainment Consultants
- Electric Contractors
- Educational Organizations
- Employment Screening Services
- Electric Materials
- Environmental & Ecological Consultants
- Electric Cars
- Electric Switches
- Elderly & Handicapped Apartments

- Energy Conservation Engineers
- Elderly & Disabled Transportation Services
- Electrolysis Schools
- Expansion Joints
- Erotic Clothing
- Entertainment Producers
- Estate Appraisal & Sales
- Educational Administration
- Electronics Schools
- Engraving Equipment
- Export Management Consultants
- Electric Tools Repair
- Educational & Textbooks
- Evaporative Coolers
- Energy Audits
- Excavation Contractors - Residential
- Express & Transfer Services
- Entertainment Agencies & Bureaus
- Electronic Instruments
- Electric Fences
- Easels
- Editorial Services
- Exotic Body Art
- Eyewear
- Energy Services
- Ear Plugs
- Eviction Services
- Excavation Contractors - Commercial & Industrial
- Exercise & Fitness Equipment
- Employment Consultants
- Electrical Discharge Machines
- Endoscopy & Laparoscopy Surgeons
- Electric Power Systems Testing & Maintenance Contractors
- Ethnic Products & Services
- Eggs Wholesale
- Electric Razors Sales & Repair
- Electronic Coils & Transformers
- Environmental Surveys
- Electronic Court Recording
- Elevator
- Earthquake Engineers
- Executive Suites & Offices
- Evidence Photographers
- Eating Disorders Counseling
- Estate Planning Insurance
- Emergency Disaster Preparedness Equipment

- Envelopes Manufacturers & Wholesalers
- Elder Law Attorneys
- Employee Benefits Consultants
- Environmental Testing Laboratories
- Environmental Services
- Estheticians
- Energy Consultants
- Embroidered Uniforms
- Electronics
- Executive Search Firms
- Enclosures & Covers Industrial
- Exporters
- Electric Fans
- Electronics Consultants
- Employment Placement Services
- Electric Transformers
- Elevator Installation, Testing, & Repair
- Erecting Contractors
- Endodontics Dentists
- Elevator Interiors
- Electronic Funds Transfer
- Employee Benefits Insurance
- Entertainers
- Emergency Services Chiropractors
- Electric Equipment Testing
- Exterior Cleaning Services

- Emergency Services
- Educational Testing Services
- Expediters
- Ear Piercing
- Embroidery Design Punching & Digitizing
- Exercise & Fitness Equipment Service & Repair
- Escrow Services
- Electronic Research, Design & Development
- Electric Cooperatives
- Engine Parts
- Elevator Shaft Cleaning
- Electric Heat Elements
- Educational Toys
- English as a Second Language Schools
- Electronic Testing Equipment Service & Repair
- Event Planning
- Earthquake Products
- Electronic Control Systems
- Exterior Shutters
- Environmental Equipment
- Etching & Engraving
- Elementary Schools
- Engineering Job Shops
- Engineering Schools
- Ear Molds
- Electrical Consultants

- Electronic Testing Equipment
- Emblems
- Estate Cleaning
- Electronic Testing
- Employee Assistance Programs Engines
- Electrolysis
- Emergency Services Dentists
- Epoxies
- Electric Motor
- Elevator Contractors - Residential
- Eye Banks
- Employee Training
- Electric Rate Consultants
- Energy Management Engineers
- Eastern Orthodox Churches
- Event Decorating Services
- Electric Motors & Generators

F

- Fishing Expeditions
- Fax Services
- Fountains
- Floor Laying Equipment
- Forklifts & Industrial Trucks Parts
- Flooring Installation & Refinishing
- Furniture Accessories

- Foundation Repair Contractors
- Furniture Movers
- Forklifts & Industrial Trucks Repair
- Fluorescent Lighting Fixtures
- Fundraising Consultants
- Facial Skin Care & Treatment
- Fruits & Vegetables
- Farm Equipment Tires
- Fence Contractors
- Fraternal Organizations Equipment
- Fashion Show Producers
- Fiber Barrels & Drums
- Felt & Felt Products
- Freight & Cargo Containers
- Football Clubs & Instruction
- Filtering Materials
- Fuel Injection Equipment
- Fire Resistant Doors
- Food & Beverage Consultants
- Fraternal Organizations
- Forensic Psychiatry Physicians
- Furniture ' Showrooms
- Freight Express & Transfer Services
- Fiber Optic Cabling
- Footwear
- Furniture Refinishing & Repair

- Floral Design Instruction
- Fruit & Vegetable Growers, Shippers, & Packers
- Fitness Consultants
- Fertilizer Handling Equipment
- Fin Coils
- Firewood
- Fuel Tanks Repair
- Fashion Designers
- Fire Departments
- Fine Art Artists
- Fire Extinguisher Recharging
- Fuel Oils Wholesale
- Foam & Sponge Rubber
- Federal Courts
- Fluid Power Valves & Hose Fittings Manufacturers
- Fishing Equipment - Commercial
- Foundries
- Fertilizer Manufacturers' Equipment
- Family Restaurants
- Fashion Design Schools
- Furniture & Fixtures Manufacturers
- Funeral Services
- Flashlights
- Funeral Information
- Filter Cleaning
- Furniture Frames & Framing
- Franchising
- Fuel Oils - Commercial
- Food Mixes
- First Aid Instruction
- Fire Brick
- Flags, Flagpoles, Banners & Pennants
- Fuel Oils
- Fundraising
- Fuel Distributors
- Fire & Water Damage Restoration-Commercial
- Fireproofing & Fire stopping Materials
- Fumigating
- Furnace Contractors
- Forensic Engineers
- Floors & Flooring
- Folding Doors
- Forestry Services
- Foundation Contractors
- Fans - Commercial & Industrial
- Fire & Water Damage Restoration Equipment
- Financial Investigators
- Fleet Insurance
- Federal Government Offices
- Foster Care Services
- Fax Software & Equipment
- Floral Wire Services
- First Aid
- Food Equipment

- Fabricated Structural Metal Manufacturers
- Fireplaces & Accessories
- Full Service Laundries
- Fuels
- Four Color Processing Printing
- Fiberglass & Materials
- Flavoring Extracts
- Flower Growers & Shippers
- Fragrances
- Franchise Consultants
- Fire Extinguishers
- Financial Guaranty & Life Insurance
- Furniture Caning Services
- Funeral Home Design Consultants
- Furnace & Air Conditioning Filters
- Furniture Designers & Custom Builders
- Fur Clothing
- Farms & Ranches Management Services
- Flower Bulbs
- Franchise & Licensing Law Attorneys
- Fruit Baskets
- Farm Produce
- Farm Equipment Service
- Flexible Metal Hose & Tubing
- Floral Consultants
- Flour Mills
- Floor Polishing, Waxing, & Cleaning Materials
- Flagstone & Slate
- Farmers' Markets
- Fruit & Vegetable
- Freight Consolidators
- Fly Fishing
- Floors & Flooring Equipment
- Floor Refinishing Supplies
- Farm Buildings
- Family Planning & Birth Control Clinics
- Floral & Balloon Arrangements
- Flatware
- Farm & Ranch Real Estate
- Fill Contractors
- Feed Concentrates & Supplements
- Farm Equipment
- Farms & Ranch Loans
- Fence Materials
- Furniture Cleaning Equipment
- Family Resorts
- Furnace Cleaning & Repair
- Fire Alarms & Monitoring Services
- Farm Equipment
- Fireworks
- Floor Resurfacing Materials
- Freight Trucking

- Forgings
- Finished Plastic Products Wholesale & Distributors
- Formica Work
- Florists
- Factory Outlets
- Food & Beverage Services
- Funeral Carrier Services
- Food Dehydrating Equipment, Supplies, & Services
- Fertilizing Services
- Fire Alarm Systems - Commercial & Industrial
- Fireplaces
- Foundations Engineers
- Funeral Equipment
- Food Processing & Manufacturers
- Foreign Marketing Consultants & Promoters
- Furriers
- Fences - Commercial
- Framed Art
- Fence
- Fiberglass & Plastic Tanks
- Forensic Accountants
- Furniture Components
- Full Gospel Churches
- Family Law Attorneys
- Full Service Moving & Storage
- Floor Machine

- Fur
- Furnished Apartments
- Fabric Outlets
- Frozen Foods
- Frozen Meats
- Fuel & Oil Filters
- Foot & Ankle Surgeons
- Financial Institutions
- Flood Zone Consultants
- French Restaurants
- Fur Consultants
- Fire Alarms Service & Repair
- Fly Fishing Equipment
- Fire & Water Damage Cleaning & Restoration
- Fishing Equipment
- Fertility Clinics
- Fundraising Merchandise
- Fur Designers & Finishers
- Fire Protection Consultants
- Food & Beverage Delivery Services
- Food Processing Equipment
- Fire Inspection & Investigations
- Futons & Accessories
- Forklift & Industrial Truck
- Fish Hatcheries
- Fabrics
- Floor Waxing, Polishing, & Cleaning - Residential

- Fireplace Equipment
- Foundation Moisture Control
- Fish Food
- Family Practice Chiropractors
- Firearm & Gun Law Attorneys
- Factories & Warehouses Real Estate
- Fire Protection Equipment Service & Repair
- Florists' Equipment
- Fireplace Cleaning Services
- Fence Posts & Accessories
- Fur Restyling & Repair
- Foreign Insurance
- Fishing Tackle Repair
- Forensic Testing Laboratories
- Food Service Consultants
- Flowers Wholesale
- Furniture Information
- Fire Alarms & Equipment Testing
- Facilities Management
- Flea Markets
- Floor Treatment & Compounds
- Financial Services
- Fire Retardant Materials
- Fertilizers
- Flanges

- Fabric Protective Treatments
- Financing Consultants
- Foundations Inspection
- Fraternities & Sororities
- Fabric Crafts
- Foam Products
- Fan Parts
- Freight Agents
- Floor Sanding
- Fine Art Photographers
- Forest Management
- Food Crops & Products
- Fertility & Infertility Physicians & Surgeons
- Flood Insurance
- Furniture Pads
- Funeral Homes & Directors
- Fire Sprinklers Maintenance
- Fire Violations Removed
- Fire Trucks
- Fiber Optic Communications
- Family Crisis Intervention Services
- Florist Information
- Fire Department Equipment
- Financial Document Information Services
- Forestry Equipment
- Financial Planning Consultants & Services

- Funeral Motor & Escort Services
- Fencing Clothing & Equipment
- Flood Control Equipment
- Funeral Alternatives
- Floor Degreasing
- Food Products
- Food Service Industrial
- Fabric Shops
- Freight Forwarding
- Foster Care Agencies
- Fishing Tournaments
- Fencing Clubs & Instruction
- Furniture Caning Supplies
- Freight & Cargo Transport
- Financial Management
- Food Service Equipment
- Forensic Consultants
- Fasteners
- Flower Preservation
- Floor Machines - Commercial
- Flood Cleanup
- Fire Extinguishers - Commercial & Industrial
- Funeral Planning
- Filing Equipment Systems
- Foam Insulation
- Furniture Covers
- Furnaces & Heating Equipment
- Fishery Consultants
- Fast Food Restaurants
- Foreign Trade & International Banks
- Fishing Docks & Piers
- Fishing
- Ferries
- First Aid Supplies
- Fences
- Fish & Wildlife Consultants
- Flags & Flagpoles
- Furniture Buyers
- Fishing Guides & Charters
- Fishing Boat Charters & Tours
- Failure Analysis Testing Laboratories
- Fulfillment Services
- Fire Sprinkler Systems - Residential
- Fax Equipment
- Fire Protection Equipment
- Fine Dining Restaurants
- Friends Churches
- Fishing Supplies & Tackle
- Factoring Services
- Forestry Consultants
- Funeral Cars
- Fiber Optic Equipment & Systems

- Fireproofing & Fire Stopping
- Fitness Clothing
- Financial Analysts Employment Agencies
- Feed & Grain
- Field Warehousing
- Floors & Flooring Contractors
- Fish & Seafood Packers
- Foursquare Gospel Churches
- Floats & Parade Supplies
- Flower Leis
- Family Planning
- Fish & Seafood Wholesale
- Fish & Seafood
- Feng Shui
- Furniture Cleaning
- Fishing Lakes Management Services
- Fire Protection Engineers
- Framing Contractors
- Fireplace & Chimney Contractors
- Fax Equipment
- Faucets
- Financial Counselors
- Fire Escapes & Exit Aids
- Fiber Optic Engineers
- Fire Sprinkler Systems
- Filtration Systems
- Fish Markets
- Fuel Suppliers
- Factory Labor Employment Agencies
- Food Trucks
- Farms & Ranches
- Frozen Food Processing
- Fur Novelties & Accessories
- Furniture Stores
- Farm Equipment & Parts
- Feed Mills Equipment
- Fruits & Vegetables Wholesale
- Fingerprint Experts
- Fire Sprinklers Testing
- Fans Repair
- Fire Alarm Sales & Service
- Financial
- Film Festivals
- Freight Traffic Consultants
- Fishing Nets
- Fire Hose
- Folding Machines
- Foreign Currency Exchange
- Fish & Chips Restaurants
- Food Processing Consultants
- Fan & Blower Parts Manufacturing
- Freight Traffic Services
- Funeral Flowers
- Foundation Drilling & Boring Contractors
- Fishing Bait & Tackle

- Fluorescent Lamps
- Fortune Tellers
- Factory Maintenance
- Furnaces
- Furniture Refinishing & Repair Equipment
- Formal Wear Sales
- Fire Hydrants
- Fans
- Fire Insurance
- Food Banks
- Fire Adjusters
- Fondue Restaurants
- Fur Cleaning & Storage
- Fax Equipment Service
- Fiberglass Repair
- Feeders
- Family Practice Physician Referrals
- Furniture
- Fiberglass Windows
- Fireplace & Chimney Building & Repair
- Furniture
- Family & General Practice Physicians & Surgeons
- Fingerprinting Services
- Folding Table
- Frozen Foods Wholesale
- Firework Displays
- Folding Tables
- Flood Assistance
- Floor Machines Service

- Farm, Crop, & Livestock Insurance

G

- Genealogy Supplies & Services
- Gas Logs
- Greek Restaurants
- Geriatric Care Nursing Homes
- Garment Bags
- Grain & Feed Transport
- Gauges
- General Surgeons
- Golf Course Consultants
- General Merchandise Wholesale
- Gold Panning
- Gear
- Gas Heating Contractors
- Gas Well Services
- Golf Guides
- Gymnasium & Track Flooring
- Golf Course Construction
- Grinding Services
- Gas & Electric Grill Parts
- Golf Driving & Practice Ranges
- Greeting Cards
- Greenhouses Equipment
- Games
- Gastroenterology Pediatrics Physicians

- Gemstones
- Gutter & Downspout Cleaning & Repair
- Grease Traps
- Golf Clothing
- Gold & Silver Plating
- Golf Equipment
- Graphics Services
- Glass, Metal, & Other Media Printing
- Glass Engraving & Etching
- Gas Equipment Industrial
- Golf Course Equipment
- Garage Equipment
- Guttering Service
- Grocery Stores & Supermarkets
- Grain Bins
- Garment Racks & Hangers
- Gates - Commercial & Industrial
- Gas Appliances Service
- Greenhouses
- Graphic Arts Schools
- Golf Tournaments
- Government Information Services
- Gun Safes
- Glass Artists
- Garbage Disposal Depots & Plants
- Geological Consultants

- General Anesthesia & Sedation Dentists
- Garbage Removal Services
- Gas Heating Equipment
- Guest Houses
- Garbage Disposals - Commercial & Industrial
- Gratings
- Graffiti Removal & Protection
- Glazing Contractors Supplies
- Garbage Disposals
- Genetics Physicians
- Gynecology & Obstetrics Physicians & Surgeons
- Gun Cases
- Gluten-Free Foods
- Gaming & Lottery
- Gold Nugget Jewelry
- Gas Engines Service & Repair
- Government Offices
- Gold, Silver, & Platinum Buyers & Sellers
- Geologists
- Guitars
- Gas Burner Parts
- Golf Outings
- Gunsmith Tools
- Group Practice Psychologists
- Government Contractors
- Gymnastics Instruction

- Gang Intervention Services
- Government Contracts & Claims Attorneys
- Granite & Marble
- Gambling Addiction Treatment Centers
- Generators - Commercial
- Gas Stove
- Golf Carts
- Gun Accessories Manufacturers
- Gift Shops
- Guard Dogs
- Geriatrics Optometrists
- Gaming Consultants
- Group Insurance
- Grease Traps & Sand Traps Service
- Gift Delivery Services
- Golf
- Gaskets
- Gift Baskets & Packs
- Guardians & Conservators
- Gas Equipment Service
- Guitar Instruction
- Gas Engines
- Grouting Contractors
- Golf Equipment Repair
- Garage Builders
- Golf Tee Times
- Gate & Fence Repair
- Gourmet Foods
- Gas Plumbing Equipment
- Gardeners
- Gospel Singing Groups
- Gutters & Downspouts
- Gas Stations Equipment Repair
- Gay & Lesbian Organizations
- Glass Rods & Tubing
- Generator
- Gas Companies
- Glass Doors
- Grinding Machines
- Grates, Grilles, Registers, & Diffusers
- Group Medical Practice
- Grocers' Wholesale
- Gas Detection & Analysis
- Gourmet Restaurants
- Gas & Water Line Installation
- Graduation Photographers
- Gowns Sales & Services
- General Practice Attorneys
- Gift Registries
- Geological Services
- Geophysicists
- Gazebo Builders
- Gymnasium Equipment
- Golf Equipment
- Gourmet Coffee
- Garbage Containers & Dumpsters
- Greek Churches

- Gas Detectors & Alarms
- Grain & Feed Handling Equipment
- Garage Floors
- Guns & Ammunition
- Gun Clubs
- Glass & Glazing Contractors
- Geographic Information Services
- Geriatric Care Management
- Granite Countertops
- Guardianship & Conservatorship Attorneys
- Grinding Tools
- Glass Bending, Beveling, Drilling, & Grinding
- Golf Carts Service & Repair
- Gift Boxes
- Geriatrics Physicians
- Gas Fireplace Piping Installation
- Granite
- Gifts & Novelties
- Global Positioning Systems
- Guns Service & Repair
- Golf Instruction
- Geriatric Consultants
- Gun Sights, Scopes, & Mounts
- Geriatrics Psychiatry Physicians
- Governor
- Geological Engineers
- Glass
- Gas Station Equipment
- Gift Certificates
- Glass Block Windows
- Gloves
- Gun Safety & Marksmanship Instruction
- Gift Wrapping Services
- General Contractors
- General Stores
- Geothermal Heating & Cooling
- Gag Gifts
- Gravel Pits
- GPS Navigation & Tracking
- Glass Replacement & Repair
- Gifts
- Graduate & Professional Schools
- Group Homes
- Greeting Card Manufacturers Supplies
- Gold & Foil Stamping
- Gas Burners Service & Repair
- Girls' Clothing
- Gift Wrap
- Gaming Centers
- Gospel Churches
- General Real Estate
- Game Meat Processing

- Gas Stations
- German Restaurants
- Geotechnical Engineers
- Garage Sales
- Gun Holsters
- Grease Duct Cleaning
- Gas Line Installation & Repair
- Glass & Glass Products
- Gauges Repair
- Grain Drying & Fumigating
- Group Practice Chiropractors
- Grading Contractors
- Global Positioning Surveyors
- Garage Organizers
- Garden Ornaments
- Glass Circles & Specialty Shapes
- Gynecology Physician Referrals
- Geothermal Drilling & Exploration
- Grocery Equipment
- Generator
- Gourmet Cooking & Bake ware
- Gymnastics Equipment
- Graduation Supplies
- Garbage Removal Contractors' Equipment
- Gypsum & Gypsum Products
- Greeting & Announcement Services
- Gas Fitters
- Game Birds & Venison
- Garbage Disposal Sales, Service, & Parts
- Greek Foods
- Gates & Operating Devices
- Gunsmiths
- Grease Collection Services
- Golf Course Architects
- Glass Furniture Tops
- Golf Communities
- Gasoline
- Gas Furnaces
- Garbage Removal Equipment
- Generator Parts Group Psychotherapy
- Guard Rails
- Garage Doors & Openers
- Gas Appliance
- Gas Fireplaces
- Garden Centers
- Gas Pipes
- Golf Associations
- Gemologists
- Gunite Contractors
- Go Carts
- Golf Courses
- Guns
- Gas & Electric Grills
- Glass Coating & Tinting – Commercial/Industrial
- Golf Tours

- Garage Door Repair
- Game Farms
- Game Development & Design
- Glass Coating & Tinting Materials
- Glass Blowers Industrial
- Gastroenterology Physicians
- Glass Gifts

H

- Horse Farms & Equipment
- Heavy Construction Equipment
- Hair Removal
- Hearing Aids
- Hair Clippers
- Honeymoon Resorts
- Helicopter Pilots & Transportation
- Heating Stoves
- Household Bar Fixtures
- Housing & Economic Development
- Humane Societies
- Holistic Health
- Hair Replacement
- Helicopter
- Hair Dryers
- House & Pontoon Boats
- Heat Pump
- Household Linens
- Hair Goods

- Hospitality Industry Education
- Housing Authorities
- Horticultural Consultants
- Health Care Consultants
- Heat Transfer Materials
- Helicopter Tours
- Heavy Hauling
- Hypnotherapy Information
- Hoisting & Rigging Equipment
- Highway Patrol
- Hazardous Waste Disposal
- Hydraulic Hoses Fabricators
- Housewares Stores
- Hunting Equipment
- Hardwood Mills
- Hot Sauces
- Horseback Riding
- Horse Shows
- Hand Painted & Crafted Furniture
- History Books
- Home Care Services
- Hotlines & Helping Lines
- Hair Supplies
- House Moving & Raising
- Health Associations
- Holiness Churches
- Health & Welfare Agencies

- Hearing Aids & Assistive Devices
- Hearing Protection
- Home Warranty Plans
- Homeopathy Physicians
- Hoisting Slings & Fittings
- Hospital Beds
- Home Improvement Information
- Heating Contractors - Commercial & Industrial
- Hair Implants & Transplants
- Hair Care Products
- Home Water Filtration Equipment
- Hydrostatic Testing
- Horse & Livestock Trailer
- Home Health Care Consultants
- Horses & Equines
- Hazardous Waste Transport
- Hospital Equipment
- Hepatology Physicians
- Hearing & Speech Rehabilitation
- Hypnotherapy Clinics
- Human Resources
- Hobbies
- Hose Coupling & Fitting
- Hand Therapy
- Homeopathy
- Hotels
- Hydraulic & Pneumatic Cylinders
- Home Theaters Custom Installation
- Horse Tack
- Household Trash Compactors
- Home Finding Services
- House Sitting
- Heavy Equipment Movers
- Homes & Residential Real Estate
- Health & Beauty Aids
- Household Portable Toilets
- Heat Exchangers
- Heating Equipment Parts
- Home Builders & Developers
- House Paint
- Housing Agencies
- Hydraulic Equipment
- Hosiery & Socks
- Heat Pump Service & Repair
- House Plans
- Health Information & Referral Consultants
- Hose Assemblies
- Hoisting & Rigging Equipment Repair
- HVAC Equipment
- Hypnosis & Hypnotherapy Schools
- Home Health Care Nurses

- Health Agencies
- Home Shopping
- Health Clubs & Gyms
- Handwriting Analysts & Experts
- Hair Accessories
- Health & Wellness Programs
- Hunting & Fishing Outfitters
- Horse Transportation
- House Cleaning
- Holistic Health Organizations
- Hotels Information
- Human Resource Consultants
- Hot Dog Restaurants
- Health Food Restaurants
- Heating & Air Conditioning Equipment
- Home Furnishings Stores
- Hindu Churches
- Handyman
- Hazardous Materials & Waste Removal
- Homeopathic Pharmacies
- Health Information
- Hat Cleaning & Blocking
- Housing Consultants
- Hunting & Fishing Licenses
- Hydraulic Pumps Repair
- Head & Neck Surgeons
- Help Desk Services

- Hotel Representatives
- Home Parties
- Hotel & Motel Reservations
- Homeowners' & Renters' Insurance
- High Tech Employment Agencies
- Hair Curlers
- Hoists, Cranes, & Monorails Manufacturers
- Hypnotherapy
- Hair Weaving
- Health Resorts
- Holistic Health Practitioners
- Hot Shot Services
- Heating Contractors
- Heat Exchanger
- Hydro mulching Services
- Home Health Care
- Horse Feed
- Health & Diet Foods
- Hand Trucks
- Hotel & Institutional Linens
- Holiday Decorations
- Household Fans
- Hunting Guides
- Home Health Care Oxygen Equipment
- Home Based Businesses
- Home Economics Consultants
- Health Care Providers

- Human Resource Management
- Hazardous Materials & Waste Services
- Home Health Care Insurance
- Hardwood
- Hawaiian Restaurants
- Headlight Cleaning
- Health Maintenance Organizations
- Hair Removal & Replacement Equipment
- Hospital Equipment
- Hardware
- Heat Treating
- Health Care Management Consultants
- Headshot & Portfolio Photographers
- Hotel & Motel Management
- Home & Building Inspection
- Home Improvement
- Horse Equipment
- Hydroponics Equipment
- Horoscopes
- Home Cooking Restaurants
- Helicopter Charter
- Hot Rod
- Hunting & Fishing Clubs
- Helium Gases
- Household Goods & Furniture Storage
- Home & Office Tanning Salons' Equipment
- Hurricane Shutters & Protection
- Headboards
- Homeless Services
- Hypnotherapy Psychiatry Physicians
- Health Care Plans
- Heating Equipment
- Hair Coloring & Tinting
- Hot & Cold Air Balloon
- Home Improvement Stores
- Hydraulic Engineers
- Hardboard
- Holistic Dentists
- Human Resource Consultant Employment Agencies
- Hospital Consultants
- Home Theaters & Entertainment Centers
- Home Schooling
- Hotel & Motel Employment Agencies
- Horticultural Plants
- Hospital Equipment Service
- Honey
- Hospitals
- Hospice Services
- Homeowners' Associations
- Home Furnishings

- Heating & Air Conditioning Service & Repair
- Hot Air Balloon Rides
- Highways & Bridges Engineers
- Hearing Aids & Assistive Devices Service & Repair
- Home Repairs & Maintenance
- Hospital & Medical Service Plans
- Household & Miscellaneous Items Plating & Replating
- Hotel & Motel Equipment
- Home Office Equipment
- Hawaiian Goods & Services
- Hand Tools
- Home Improvement Loans
- Horse & Carriage Rides
- Helicopters Service & Repair
- Home Equity Loans
- Hematology Physicians
- Hostels
- Hotels & Motels Developers
- Holistic Health Physicians
- Hookah Bars & Restaurants

- Health Care Law Attorneys
- Historical Places & Services
- Hearing Aid Specialists
- Heating Radiators
- Hand Blown Glass
- Hand Surgeons
- Health Insurance
- Hunting & Fishing Information Services
- Hematology & Oncology Pediatrics Physicians
- Hay & Alfalfa Products
- Hydraulic Hoses & Fittings
- Historical Research
- Heating & Air Conditioning Contractors
- HVAC Contractors
- Hose & Tubing
- Hockey Equipment
- Human Relations Consultants
- Housing Projects
- Hazardous Materials & Waste Equipment
- Hotel & Motel Consultants
- Hydraulic Equipment Service & Repair
- Heating Equipment & Systems
- Home Theater Services
- Heating & Ventilating Contractors

- Hydro seeding Services
- Homes & Institutions
- Hot Springs
- Health Spas
- Home Design
  & Planning Services
- Health Education
- Hunting & Fishing
  Lodges
- Holistic Health
  Information Services
- Hobby & Model Stores
- Home Decorating
  Supplies
- Historical Organizations
- Hobby & Model
  Supplies
- Horse Care
  & Management
- Holding Companies
- Herbs
- Heating Equipment
  & Systems Cleaning
  & Repair
- Heating Stove
  Installation
- Heavy Duty Towing
- Hair Loss Clinics
- Handbags
- Health Care
  Professionals
- Herbalists
- Household Goods
  Moving & Storage
- HVAC Engineers
- Housing Assistance
- Horseshoers

- Hydraulic Oils
- Heating & Air
  Conditioning Parts
- Hula Instruction
- Health Care Computer
  Applications
- Hydraulic Tools
- Housewares
- Hockey Clubs
  & Instruction
- Handicap Accessible
  Building Modification
- Home Automation
  Systems
- Heating Equipment -
  Commercial & Industrial
- Heavy Construction
- Hair Braiding
- Hearing Aid
  Audiologists
- Health Food Stores
- Hazardous Materials
  & Waste Contractors
- Health Care
  Management
- Horse Trailers
- High Schools
- Hats & Caps
- Home Playground
  Equipment
- Hides & Furs
- Human Relations
  & Career Coaching
- Hazardous Materials
  & Waste Engineers
- Headlight Adjustment

- Household Pump Installation
- Halitosis Dentists
- Horseshoer's Equipment
- Helium Balloon Tanks
- Hypnotists Entertainers
- Hydrologists
- Herbs Wholesale
- Hunting & Fishing Preserves
- Hay Rides & Sleigh Rides
- Home & Recreational Generators
- Hunting
- Horse Riding Schools
- Hiking Boots
- Hydraulic Seals
- Heat Exchangers Service
- Hand & Power Tools
- Hot Water Heat Contractors
- Handbags Repair
- Hospitalization Insurance
- Human Resource Development Training
- Home Health Care Equipment
- Heaters
- Hazardous Materials & Waste Consultants
- Hyperbaric Services

- Historical Preservation & Restoration Services
- Hydroponics

- Home Child Care
- Hunan Restaurants
- Horse Breeders
- Humidifiers
- Horse Trainers
- Heavy Construction Equipment Repair
- Hair Care & Treatment

I

- Internet Monitoring Software
- Insurance Claims & Services
- Ignition Interlock Devices
- Ice Skating Rinks & Instruction
- International Restaurants
- Italian Foods
- Insulation Materials
- Invitation Printing
- Insect Control Devices
- Insurance Agents
- Italian Restaurants
- Insurance Services
- Internet Development
- Industrial Shredders
- Irrigation Ditch Contractors
- Ice Makers
- Identification Records Services
- Insulation Consultants
- Internet Directories
- Insurance Adjusters

- Insurance Claims Processing Services
- Immigration & Naturalization Consultants
- Inventors
- Inspection & Testing Engineers
- Irrigation Consultants
- Ice Cream Cones
- Interior Design Schools
- Indian Restaurants
- Interior Finish Out Contractors
- Insecticides
- Independent Churches
- Incense & Potpourri
- Interior Designers' Supplies
- Investments
- Industrial Engineers
- Industrial Parks
- Industrial Tapes
- Identification Equipment
- Infrared Equipment & Services
- Indexing & Abstracting Services
- Internet Publishing
- Income Tax Consultants
- Industrial & Trade Schools
- Ice
- Immigration Law Attorneys
- Irrigation Pumps

- Interior Landscaping
- Iron Work Welding
- Indonesian Restaurants
- Industrial Consultants
- Iron Work Machinery
- Image Processing Equipment & Systems
- Industrial Equipment
- Insulation Contractors
- Ice cream Manufacturers Equipment
- Inks
- Interior Plants Design
- Importers
- Industrial Unions
- Inverters
- Industrial Equipment
- Insurance Annuities
- Invention Marketing Services
- Industrial Control Instruments
- Internet Domain Registration & Brokering
- Irrigation, Fertilizing, & Spraying Equipment
- Industrial & Marine Cleaning Services
- Independent Fee Appraisers
- Insulated Wire & Cable
- Insurance Underwriters
- Identification Equipment Manufacturers
- Identification Cards & Badges

- Ice Makers Service & Repair
- Imported Foods
- Illustrators
- Internet Security Services
- Industrial Contractors
- Insulation Materials - Commercial & Industrial
- Interior Decorators' & Designers' Workrooms
- Ice Cream & Frozen Desserts
- Institutional Uniforms
- Insurance Examiners
- Information Search & Retrieval Service
- Inspection Services
- Illustrations
- Industrial & Construction Fasteners
- International Movers
- Industrial Tool
- Individual & Family Services Organizations
- Interactive Advertising
- Indoor Golf Courses
- Investment Management
- Incentive Travel
- Indoor Advertising
- Individual Counseling
- Internet Cafes
- Internet Consultants
- Instrumentation Engineers
- Interior Decorators & Designers
- Invitations & Announcements
- Indoor & Outdoor Courts Construction
- Independent Researchers
- Institutional Libraries
- Internet Marketing Services
- Internet Access Software
- Insured Property Replacement Services
- Insurance Examinations
- Insurance Employment Agencies
- Image Consultants
- Irrigation Equipment Service
- International Affairs
- Insurance Retirement Annuities & Pension
- Industrial Maintenance Contractors
- Information Systems Consultants
- Inventory Control Systems
- Industrial & Medical Gases
- Irrigation Equipment
- Industrial Containers
- Industrial Lift
- Interactive Media Services
- Ice Sculptures

- Information Processing Equipment & Systems
- Industrial Design Consultants
- Institutional Food
- Insulation Contractors - Residential
- Income Tax Services
- Immunizations
- Internet Databases
- Intermediate Care Nursing Homes
- Industrial & Medical Gas
- Information Bureaus
- Internet Software Design
- Investment Services
- International Law Attorneys
- Ice Skate Sharpening & Repairing
- Insurance Law Attorneys
- Ice Melting Equipment
- Insulation Removal
- Investment Bankers
- Indian Goods Wholesale & Manufacturing
- Investigators
- Industrial Water Heaters
- Internal Medicine Veterinarians
- Insurance Bonds
- Internal Medicine Physicians
- Image Processing
- Imported Rug
- Imaging Service Bureaus
- Irrigation Associations
- Industrial Drying Equipment
- Interior Building Cleaning
- Industrial Computer
- Internet Products & Services
- Irish Restaurants
- Independent Living Services
- Inflatables
- Industrial Fabrics
- Induction Heating Equipment
- Interdenominational Churches
- Internet Training
- Internet Management
- Internet Service Providers
- Indoor Playgrounds
- Insurance Inspection Services
- Incorporation Services
- Intellectual Property Attorneys
- Industrial Saws
- Insurance
- International Business Services
- Ice Cream & Frozen Mixes
- Insulating Windows
- Investment Promotion Agencies
- Insurance Information

- Internet Services
- Iron & Steel
- Ice Makers & Dispensers Equipment
- Iranian Restaurants
- Interior Decorators
- Indoor Baseball & Softball Facilities
- Interior Cleaning Services
- Investment Advisory Services
- International Mailing & Shipping Services
- Inspection Devices Industrial
- Internet Advertising
- Intercom Systems & Service
- Inventory Services
- Information Technology Services
- Instrumental Music Instruction
- Industrial Equipment Rebuilding, Service, & Repair
- Instructional Materials
- Industrial Furnaces
- Ice Cream & Frozen Yogurt Shops
- Insects
- Iron & Steel Stairs
- Immigration & Naturalization
- Irrigation Sprinkler Designers
- Internet Database Management Services
- Insulation Contractors Equipment
- International Trade Consultants
- Investment Securities
- International Marketing
- Interlocking Bricks & Pavers
- Infrared Spectroscopy Testing Laboratories
- Impregnating
- Insurance Plan Administrators
- Ice Cream Freezers Sales, Service, & Parts
- Industrial Hygiene Consultants
- Identity Theft Services
- Image & Graphics Printing
- Insurance Consultants & Advisors
- Infectious Disease Physicians & Surgeons
- Industrial Equipment & Machinery Training
- Ice Wholesale
- Investors
- Individual Retirement Accounts
- Indoor Air Quality

J

- Jackets & Suits
- Japanese Restaurants
- Jewish Books
- Jewelry Design Schools
- Job Listing Services
- Junior High & Middle Schools
- Jigs & Fixtures
- Jewelry Display Cases
- Junior Colleges & Technical Institutes
- Jewelry
- Jewelers' Equipment
- Janitorial Contractors Information
- Jacks
- Jewelry Designers
- Junk
- Jewelry Repair
- Jewelry Mountings
- Jewelers
- Jewelry Engravers
- Jackets
- Janitorial Equipment
- Juice Bars
- Jury & Trial Consultants
- Jewish Schools
- Jewelry & Buyers
- Juvenile Law Attorneys
- Jewish Goods
- Jet Propelled Skis Service
- Jewelry Appraisers
- Jeans
- Janitorial Services

- Jamaican Restaurants
- Jewish Synagogues
- Jewel Setters
- Junk Removal
- Japanese Foods
- Justices of the Peace
- Jukebox Services
- Jewelry Contractors
- Jet Propelled Ski
- Junk Car Removal
- Judges
- Jet Propelled Skis

K

- Knit Fabrics
- Kitchen Consultants
- Kennel Equipment
- Knobs
- Korean Churches
- Kitchen Equipment Refinishing
- Keyboards Musical Instruments
- Key makers
- Kitchen Cabinets & Equipment
- Kites & Gliders
- Knitting & Crocheting
- Knee Surgeons
- Kosher Foods
- Kitchen Fixtures
- Kitchen & Bathroom Remodeling
- Kitchen Cabinet Re-facing
- Kilns

- Kosher Caterers
- Kerosene
- Karate, Judo, & Kung Fu Instruction
- Kosher Restaurants
- Karaoke
- Karaoke Restaurants
- Key Control Systems
- Kitchen Equipment - Commercial
- Korean Foods
- Kitchen Design & Remodeling Services
- Knitting Machines
- Kitchen Gifts & Accessories
- Kitchen Accessories
- Knives & Cutlery
- Kitchenware & Glassware
- Korean Restaurants
- Keys
- Kinesiology Chiropractors
- Kitchen Exhaust System Cleaning
- Karaoke Machine Sales,
- Karaoke Clubs
- Kennels
- Karaoke Equipment
- Kiosks
- Knitting & Crocheting Accessories
- Kitchen Cabinet Remodeling

L

- Lawn Mower Sharpening Equipment
- Long Term Care Facilities
- Lumber Services
- Lamps & Lamp Shades
- Lathes
- Land Planning
- Letter Shop Services
- Leather Clothing Cleaning
- Loss Prevention Services
- Large Animal Veterinarians
- Lot Cleaning Contractors
- Lasers
- Locks & Locksmiths - Commercial & Industrial
- Learning Disabilities Evaluation & Consultation
- Ladder
- Llama & Alpaca Farms
- Laundries
- Lawn & Garden Equipment
- Livestock Feeding Services
- Lighting - Commercial
- Ladders
- Lighting Fixtures
- Landlord & Tenant Law Attorneys
- Legal Research & Support Services

- Legal Secretarial Schools
- Living Plant Rentals
- Landscape Installation
- Legal Consultants
- Lapidaries
- Laser Printers Service
- Laser Printer Supplies
- Legal Assistance
- Labor Unions
- Lightning Protection Equipment
- Lawn & Garden Services
- Local Trucking
- Lubricating Oils Distributors
- Lawn Spraying & Treatment
- Leak Repair Contractors
- Lamp Shades Cleaning, Repairing, & Recovering
- Lawn & Garden Equipment
- Landscape - Commercial Maintenance
- Light Bulbs & Tubes
- Lighting Consultants
- LAN/WAN Devices
- License Plate Frames
- Laces
- Lamp Shades
- Lunch Restaurants
- Lumber
- Lamps
- Landfills & Transfer Stations

- Library Management & Research
- Land Contracts
- Livestock Equipment
- Lubricating Greases
- Labor Relations Consultants
- Legal Graphics
- Legal Photographers
- Legal Services
- Log & Lumber Hauling
- Liquid & Bulk Storage
- Landscape Architects
- Logos
- Laminating Products
- Learning Disabilities
- Land Companies
- Lamp Mounting & Repair
- Lawn & Garden Tractors
- Loose Leaf Binders
- Landscape Designers
- Lighting Equipment & Systems
- Liability & Malpractice Insurance
- Land Surveyors - Commercial
- Law Enforcement Training
- Lemon Law Attorneys
- Lawn Mower Parts
- Legal Clinics
- Landscape Gardeners
- Laboratory Equipment Service & Repair

74

- Limousine Customizing
- Learning Disability Counseling
- Local Bus Charters
- Live Theater
- Leather Craft Supplies
- Labels & Tags
- Laminating Services - Commercial
- Licensed Practical Nurses LPN
- Landscape Contractors Information & Referral
- Legal Copying Services
- Legal Counsel & Prosecution
- Livestock Producers
- Lawn Mowers
- Laminating Equipment
- Lead Detection & Removal - Residential
- Landscape Nurserymen
- Laptop Computers
- Label & Tag Printing
- Lubricating Oils
- Liquefied Petroleum Gas Bottled & Bulk
- Logistics
- Liquidators
- Lawn & Garden Outdoor Power Equipment
- Leak Detecting Instruments
- Lawn Ornaments & Decorations
- Leather Goods Trimmings
- Leather Clothing
- Lighting Plants
- Lawn Maintenance Equipment
- Lead & Lead Products
- Low Vision Aids
- Lake & Pond Construction
- Late Night Restaurants
- Landscape Designers - Commercial
- Log Splitting Equipment
- Luggage Carriers
- Livestock Auctions
- Low Voltage Systems Contractors
- Lithographers
- Linoleum
- Licensed Psychologists
- Litigation Support Consultants
- Lawn & Garden Sprinklers
- Legal Documents Assistance
- Lobbyists
- Lawn Mower Sharpening
- Liposuction Surgeons
- Lakes
- Lake & Beach Cleaning
- Laser Game Centers
- Lapidary Equipment
- Legal Secretaries Employment Agencies
- Lake Management Services

- Landscape Equipment
- Lightning Rods
- Lawn & Irrigation Sprinklers
- Lighting Engineers
- Log Homes, Buildings, & Cabins
- Lawn & Garden Sprinklers Parts
- Louvers
- Livestock Equipment
- Locksmith
- Lie Detectors
- Lighting Fixture Parts
- Luggage Repair
- Licensed Contractors
- Lutheran Schools
- Law Enforcement
- Leather Goods
- Leaded Art Glass
- Laser Surgeons
- Letter Signs
- Laser Entertainment
- Livestock Transport
- Life Insurance
- Lawn Consultants
- Lottery Tickets
- Landscape Lighting
- Lawn & Garden Chemicals
- Log Furniture
- Lumber Mill Representatives
- Limousine Services
- Lawn Mowing - Commercial
- Lime & Limestone
- Locksmiths' Equipment
- Landlord Service Bureaus
- Landscape Services
- Livestock
- Laundry Equipment - Commercial Service & Repair
- Light Duty Trucking
- Lighting Contractors
- Lawn Care Supplies
- Lawn Services
- Livestock Breeders
- Lift Trucks
- Laboratories
- Limousine Information
- Latin American Restaurants
- Lumber Treating & Drying
- Landscape Contractors - Commercial & Industrial
- Legal Marketing Services
- Local Government Offices
- Lockers
- Lubricants
- Lighting Fixtures Repair, Maintenance & Installation
- Loggers
- Liquefied Petroleum Gas
- Leather Goods Equipment
- Linoleum Contractors

- Legal Forms
- Lacquers
- Laboratory Equipment
- Language Schools & Instruction
- Laundry Equipment Service
- Lake Resorts
- Liquor License Consultants
- Lodges
- Lebanese Restaurants
- Language Training Aids
- Landscaping Stone
- Louvered Windows
- Lathing Contractors
- Liquor Stores
- Luggage Stores
- Lighting Equipment & Systems
- Landscape Foresters
- Laboratory Furniture
- Lubricants & Lubricating Compounds
- Lien Processing & Registration Service
- Lawn Mower
- Land Surveyors
- Laundry Equipment
- Lutheran Churches
- Lawn Mowing Services
- Leather Findings & Finishes
- Laminated Structural Products
- Labeling Equipment
- Log Siding
- Long Distance Phone Service
- Low Vision Eyeglasses
- Latex & Latex Products
- Laser Cosmetic Treatments
- Laser Therapy
- Lifeguard Services
- Labor Relations Counselors
- Loan & Financing Services
- Lifts Industrial Repair & Parts
- Laser Vision Correction
- Lawn & Garden Sprinklers Installation & Service
- Laser Hair Removal
- Local Phone Services
- Laser Printers
- Legal Video Services
- Laser Cutting
- Libraries
- Land Use & Zoning Attorneys
- Legal Information Services
- Learning Disabilities Information Services
- Landscape Curbing
- Lawn Leveling & Seeding Services
- Licensed Plumbing Contractors

- Land Preparation
  Contractors
- Lawn & Garden
  Furnishings
- Liquid & Dry Bulk
  Trucking
- Lawn & Garden
  Sprinklers - Commercial
- Licensed Massage
  Therapists
- Land Clearing
  & Leveling Contractors
- Lacrosse Equipment
- Lighting
- Leak Detection Services
- Leather Bound Books
- Lighting Maintenance
- LPG Home Delivery
- Leather Furniture
- Lactation Consultants
- Log & Timber Buyers
- Logging & Lumber
  Equipment
- Learning Centers
- Loan Schedules
- Legal Service Plans
- Landscape Architects -
  Commercial & Industrial
- Loading Dock
  Equipment
- Lie Detection Services
- Lobsters
- Lawn Maintenance -
  Commercial & Industrial
- Locks & Locksmiths
- Loan

- Liquid Filters
- Lawn Installation
  & Maintenance Services
- Letterhead & Envelope
  Printing
- Legal Forms Preparation
  Services
- Lubricating Devices,
  Equipment, & Systems
- Land Development
  & Planning Engineers
- Lecture & Seminar
  Services
- Liquor Delivery Services
- Law Schools
- Luggage
- Landscape Contractors
- Labor Organizations
- Licensed Public
  Accountants
- Legal & Financial
  Printing
- Linen Supply

M

- Mining Equipment
  Repair
- Marine Engines
  & Transmissions
- Men's Organizations
- Music Printers
- Mental Health
- Meat Lockers
- Moving Equipment

- Materials Handling Equipment Service & Repair
- Medical & Infectious Waste Removal
- Mortgage Feasibility Consultants
- Medical Technical Services
- Medical Equipment
- Maps & Globes
- Music Festivals
- Moving & Storage Consultants
- Medical Bills Auditing Services
- Metal Processing & Fabricating Equipment
- Mosaics
- Milling Machines
- Mountain Bike Off Road Trails
- Marketing Programs
- Microwave Communications Equipment & Systems
- Major Appliance Repair
- Mattress Renovating
- Magicians' & Jugglers' Equipment
- Mammography Information
- Mobile Home Anchoring
- Modular Home
- Mortgage Refinancing
- Maids & Butlers
- Medical Collection Services
- Mirrors
- Mufflers & Exhaust Systems
- Metaphysicians
- Medicine Cabinets
- Movers
- Machine Tool
- Major Appliance Parts
- Mobile Home Set Up & Tear Down
- Men's Uniforms
- Motorcycles & Motor Scooters
- Medical Books
- Motorized Escort Services
- Materials Handling Consultants
- Municipal Courts
- Marine Cargo & Freight
- Model Trains
- Medicare Supplemental & Long Term Care Insurance
- Motorcycle Riding & Safety Instruction
- Market Research
- Metal Stamping
- Multimedia
- Military Schools
- Metal Detectors
- Machine Tools Rebuilding
- Medical Secretarial Schools

- Marine Wildlife Encounters
- Motorcycle Consignment
- Mail Order Fulfillment Services
- Mining Development
- Meats
- Memory Improvement Training
- Meat Cutting Services
- Motor Scooters & Mini bikes Parts
- Malt & Hops
- Motion Picture Stock Shots
- Metal Distributors
- Missionary Churches
- Marine Fiberglass Service
- Metal Windows
- Medical & Dental Photographers
- Metal Bed Frames
- Mugs
- Mini Blinds
- Miniature Golf Courses
- Miners
- Moving & Storage
- Military & Veterans Organizations
- Malpractice & Negligence Attorneys
- Motion Picture Casting Services
- Major Appliance
- Medical Billing Software

- Metal Roofs & Siding
- Martial Arts Equipment
- Mobile Home Parks & Communities
- Medical & Dental X-Ray Laboratories
- Medicinal & Botanicals
- Myofunctional Therapists
- Mothproofing
- Manicures & Pedicures
- Molds
- Missing Persons Organizations
- Magazine Subscription Agents
- Masonry Contractors - Commercial & Industrial
- Motorcycles & ATVs Service & Repair
- Mold & Mildew Prevention, Inspection, & Removal
- Marketing Consultants
- Metal Cutting Machines
- Mobile Medical Diagnostic Equipment
- Marine Equipment Service
- Mining Equipment
- Metal Tubes & Tubing
- Mirrored Doors
- Marine Electric Contractors
- Machine Shop Equipment Industrial
- Motorized Carts

- Medical Billing Services
- Mailing Services
- Machine Knives
- Midwives
- Multimedia Services
- Maxillofacial Physicians
- Mini & Self Storage
- Magnetic Signs
- Mathematicians
- Microphones
- Marine Electronics
- Motion Picture Sound Services
- Manuscript Services
- Military Bases & Units
- Medical Personnel Employment Agencies
- Massage & Bodywork
- Metallurgists
- Mini & Self Storage Warehouses
- Multimedia Software
- Medical Testing
- Mannequins
- Marine Surveyors & Adjustors
- Mobile Offices & Commercial Units
- Motorcycles & Motor Scooters Parts
- Marking & Coding Equipment & Systems
- Mortgage Service Bureaus
- Motion Picture Set Design
- Magnets & Magnetic Devices
- Model Car Racing Centers
- Music Downloads
- Masonry Contractors
- Marble Vanity Tops
- Music Venues
- Marketing & Public Relations
- Motion Picture Film Archives
- Microscopes
- Musician
- Mortuary Transportation Services
- Moving Labor Services
- Marine Shells
- Mezzanines & Platforms Equipment & Systems
- Masonry Buildings
- Mobile Home Roofing
- Management Accountants
- Marble Tiles
- Motorcycles Tires
- Mobile Home Equipment & Parts
- Monogramming & Initialing Machines
- Merchandise Marts
- Metal Products
- Motorcycle Inspection
- Metal Cleaning
- Mechanical Seals

- Map Designers, Publishers & Distributors
- Middle Eastern Restaurants
- Millwork
- Metal Tiles
- Management Engineers
- Mortgages Information
- Marine Transportation Consultants
- Mufflers & Exhaust Service & Repair
- Mobile Home Site Preparation
- Metal Specialties
- Medical Legal Consultants
- Music Stores
- Mobile Auto Oil & Lube
- Metal Buildings
- Monuments & Markers
- Musical Instrument Parts
- Metal Drilling
- Minor Medical Emergency Services
- Manicures & Pedicures Equipment
- Marking & Coding Services
- Military Recruiting
- Medical Examinations
- Mobile Pet Services
- Metal Spinning
- Moroccan Restaurants
- Mosques
- Mailing Equipment

- Motorcycle Campers & Trailers
- Medical Records & Billing Schools
- Miniature Shops
- Mattresses
- Mobile Home Listings
- Mammography Clinics
- Metal Forming Machinery
- Maternity Clothing
- Men's Clothing
- Measuring Instrument
- Microfilm Storage
- Marine Equipment
- Mobile & Modular Home Washing & Cleaning
- Marine Engineers
- Metal Sculptures
- Mortgages - Commercial
- Music Libraries
- Mental Health Counselors
- Medical Services
- Medical Research Physicians & Surgeons
- Medical Imaging
- Medical Research
- Mailing List Services
- Marine Construction
- Mobile Homes Transporting
- Microwave Ovens Service
- Marketing Sales

- Motorcycles & Motor Scooters Trails & Tracks
- Music Teachers
- Metal Stamping Equipment
- Metal Roofing Contractors
- Malaysian Restaurants
- Martial Arts Instruction
- Military & Veterans Law
- Magicians
- Managed Care Plans
- Metal Recycling
- Meter Boxes
- Military Supplies
- Mental Health Practitioners
- Mortuaries
- Mailboxes
- Meditation Organizations
- Mortgage Companies
- Medical Claims Processing
- & Assistance
- Materials Handling Engineers
- Mortgage Loan Reduction
- Metal Art
- Motels
- Marine Engines & Drive Trains Repair
- Mobile Home Inspection
- Medical & Infectious Waste Disposal
- Motion Picture Producers & Studios
- Metal Coating & Allied Services
- Marine Service Stations
- Marine Contractors
- Market Research Consultants
- Manufacturing
- Meat Choppers & Grinders
- Metal Finishing
- Machine Shops
- Medical Schools
- Men's Neckwear
- Meat Rendering
- Motorcycles Transport
- Mastectomy Supplies
- Mutual Fund Insurance
- Maternity Homes
- Misting Fans & Systems
- Musical Instruments Service
- Major Electric Appliance
- Minerals & Mining
- Motorcycle Performance & Racing Equipment
- Mongolian Restaurants
- Medical Imaging Equipment
- Modeling Agencies
- Medical Laboratories
- Mental Health Agencies
- Marine Salvage
- Music Distributors

- Medical Office Buildings Management
- Moldings
- Mechanical Engineers
- Meats Wholesale
- Motion Picture Film Servicing
- Medical Emergency Notification Services
- Moving & Storage Equipment
- Moped
- Marine Refrigeration & Air Conditioning Sales & Service
- Mobile Homes
- Motorcycle Machine Shop Services
- Medical Laboratory Schools
- Meat Processing Equipment
- Metal Cabinets
- Metal Slitting & Shearing
- Motion Picture Services
- Model Makers
- Moving Boxes
- Mobile Home
- Municipal & Corporate Bonds
- Multi-Level Marketing
- Marine Propulsion Systems
- Mapping & Topographical Services
- Medical Diagnostic Clinics
- Myotherapy
- Musical Instruments
- Mobile Health Care
- Meal Preparation
- Mobile Auto Service & Repair
- Music Boxes
- Mirror Hanging Service
- Minerals & Ores
- Multimedia Presentations
- Metal Refiners & Smelters
- Manufacturers' Agents & Representatives
- Marine Hardware
- Mobile Home Manufacturers' Equipment & Parts
- Music Instruction
- Metal Specialties Manufacturers
- Media Consultants
- Major Appliances
- Mobile Auto Key & Remote Replacement
- Mausoleum Builders
- Marine Coatings
- Metal Furniture
- Music Workshops
- Mechanical Engravers
- Mergers & Acquisitions
- Music & Recording Industry

- Major Appliance Refinishing
- Model Airplanes
- Mexican & Latin American Goods
- Mediterranean Restaurants
- Mobile Home Service, Repair, & Improvements
- Music
- Modeling & Charm Schools
- Metal Machine Parts Manufacturers
- Microwave Oven
- Marriage & Family Counseling Information
- Marine Professionals
- Modular Offices
- Millinery
- Mirror Re-silvering
- Medical Equipment Service
- Manufactured & Mobile Homes
- Manufacturing Engineers
- Menu Printing
- Music Composers' Agents
- Mobile Home
- Mud Jacking Contractors
- Mini Cars
- Mountain & Rock Climbing Instruction
- Metalworking Equipment
- Music Production Consultants
- Metal Cutting
- Machine Shafting
- Motorcycles & Scooters Painting & Customizing
- Movers Information
- Mixing & Agitation Machinery
- Musical Instrument
- Monuments & Markers Cleaning
- Ministries Churches
- Meat Processing
- Mortgages
- Movie Theaters
- Marine Propellers Sales
- Motorcycles Insurance
- Merchandise
- Marriage Officiates
- Medical & Dental Assistant & Technician Schools
- Marine Fuel
- Makeup Consultants & Studios
- Mobile Home Parks Development & Construction
- Masquerade & Theatrical Costumes Sales
- Media Buyers
- Music Producers
- Motorcycle Clothing
- Motion Picture Production Services & Facilities

- Musicians
- Metal Finishing Equipment
- Massage Equipment
- Medicare
- Meat Packers
- Mobile Home Financing
- Municipal Engineers
- Mexican Foods
- Marine Radar, Radio, & Telephone
- Metaphysical Books
- Materials Handling Equipment
- Music Therapy
- Medical Records Management
- Mantels
- Mission Churches
- Motion Picture Laboratories
- Mats & Matting
- Meters
- Masonry Equipment
- Meat Packers Wholesale
- Music Publishers
- Mechanical Contractors
- Media
- Music Management
- Motion Picture Special Effects
- Motion Picture Projection Services
- Men's Shirts
- Mailing Machines & Equipment Wholesale
- Mail Receiving & Forwarding
- Management Consultants
- Mortgage
- Mail Order & Catalog Sales
- Mobile Home Insurance
- Music Composers' Supplies
- Millwrights
- Monuments & Markers Manufacturing Equipment
- Medical Reimbursement Services
- Metal
- Music Composers & Arrangers
- Massage Schools
- Metal Fabricators
- Marking Dies
- Musical Instruments Supplies
- Metaphysical Churches
- Men's Accessories
- Mortgage Insurance
- Machinery Movers & Erectors
- Microscope Repair
- Machine Tools Wholesale
- Motion Picture Film
- Minerals, Oil, & Gas Investments
- Mail Services & Package Shipping
- Mining Consultants

- Mops
- Metal Doors, Sash, & Trim
- Murals Artists
- Money
- MRI
- Motion Picture Equipment
- Metals
- Movie Collectibles
- Major Electric Appliances Repair & Parts
- Mosquito Control
- Marine Electronics Service
- Medical Alarms
- Medical Spas
- Marine Stereo Systems
- Metal Door Frames
- Metal Finishing Laboratories
- Metal Buildings Maintenance & Repair
- Music Rehearsal Studios
- Metal Building Contractors
- Marine Upholstery - Commercial & Industrial
- Millwork Contractors
- Mexican Restaurants
- Mountain & Rock Climbing Equipment
- Manholes & Manhole Covers
- Management Training
- Mausoleums

- Metal Shaping
- Motorized Bicycles
- Marinas
- Men's Health Physicians
- Money Orders & Transfer Services
- Mirrors - Commercial
- Moving & Storage - Commercial & Industrial
- Methodist Churches
- Marketing Agencies
- & Counselors
- Mulch
- Messianic Synagogues
- Mental Health Clinics
- Meditation Instruction
- Metal Polishing, Buffing, & Plating
- Medical Diagnostic Services
- Mathematics Schools
- Metallurgical Testing Laboratories
- Mortgage Loan Processing
- Metal Tanks
- Marble Decorators
- Marionettes & Puppets
- Merchandising Services
- Murals & Faux Finishes
- Masquerade & Theatrical Make Up
- & Development Consultants
- Mortgage & Loan Banks

- Medical Malpractice Attorneys
- Metal Spraying
- Monuments & Markers Lettering
- Magazine & Periodical Advertising
- Marble & Terrazzo Cleaning
- Maid & Butler Registries
- Mechanical Packing Materials
- Motion Picture Equipment Service & Repair
- Medical Transcription
- Marble Contractors
- Mining Engineers
- Mutual Funds
- Medical Equipment
- Milk & Milk Products
- Maritime & Admiralty Law Attorneys
- Materials Testing Laboratories
- Meditation & Relaxation Products & Services
- Metaphysical & Occult Supplies
- Motor Oils & Greases
- Men's Shoes
- Magazine & Journal Publishers
- Music Production
- Mountain & Ice Climbing Tours
- Mailbox

- Medical & Surgical Emergency Services
- Masquerade & Novelty Masks
- Moss Removal & Control
- Money Market Funds
- Microbreweries
- Marriage Record
- Metal Castings
- Motion Picture Editing Services
- Metal Coatings
- Medical Services Organizations
- Microfilming & Imaging Service Equipment
- Milk & Milk Products Wholesale
- Medical Research Centers
- Marine & River Terminals
- Meter Repair
- Montessori Schools
- Metal Rolling & Forming
- Men's Custom Jackets & Suits
- Motivational Speakers
- Marriage & Family Counseling
- Museums
- Marriage Records
- Media & Communications Law Attorneys

N

- Nail Salon Equipment
- Nutritionists
- Neuropsychological Testing
- Novelty Jewelry
- Naturopathic Physicians
- Newsletters
- Notions
- Nephrology Pediatrics Physicians & Surgeons
- Nutrition Consultants
- Nail Care
- Name Plate Manufacturers
- Nightclub Information Services
- Nozzles
- Nutrition Centers
- Non-Certified Public Accountants
- News & Sports Services
- Natural & Cut Stone
- Neurology Pediatrics Physicians & Surgeons
- Nails, Tacks, & Staples
- Newsletter Printing
- Native American Law Attorneys
- Newspaper Feature Syndicates
- Non-Ceramic Tile Contractors
- Nephrology Physicians
- Neurology Physicians
- Nurses' Aides

- Name Plates & Tags
- Network Marketing
- Non-Sports Trading Cards
- Noodles
- Nuts
- Notary Public Schools
- Non-Cellular Mobile Phone Service
- New Testament Churches
- Nurses Registered Professional RN
- Navigation & Marine Instruction
- Nailing Machinery
- Naturotherapists
- Neuropsychiatry Psychiatry Physicians
- Nursing Homes Consultants
- Neurology Veterinarians
- Numerologists
- Nuclear Services
- Non-Profit Accountants
- Nurserymen's Equipment
- Nurse Midwives
- Network Consultants
- Natural Stone Flooring
- Nursing Schools
- Newsletter & Small Publication Production Services
- Nutrition Physicians
- Naturopathic Clinics
- Nail Care Products

- Nursing & Convalescent Homes
- Newspaper Publishers
- Non-Ceramic Tiles
- Neurology Chiropractors
- Nuts Wholesale & Processing
- Native American Art Galleries
- Neurology Surgeons
- News & News stands
- Newspaper Delivery
- Novelties
- Natural Healing Products
- Nursing & Personal Care Facilities
- Notary & Corporation Seals
- Non-Denominational Churches
- Nurserymen Equipment
- Nondestructive Testing Laboratories
- Nursing Homes Information & Placement
- Native American Goods
- Neon Novelties
- Non-Prescription Medicines
- Native Crafts
- Nursing Supplies
- Newspaper Correspondents
- Novelty Signs
- Neonatology Physicians
- Nurses & Registries
- Natural Marble
- Nonprofit Organizations Attorneys
- Noise Control Consultants
- Notaries Public
- Nightclubs
- Nursing Homes Management
- Nutrition Programs
- Native American Arts & Crafts
- Neon Signs
- National Security
- Nurse Practitioners
- Natural Stone Wholesale
- Nannies
- New American Restaurants
- Nuclear Medicine Physicians & Surgeons
- Non-Emergency Ambulance Services
- National Parks & Landmarks
- Nurses Recruiting
- Nudist Parks & Resorts
- Nurses
- Nutrition Chiropractors
- New Auto Pre-Delivery Service
- Network Solutions
- Natural Granite & Marble
- Natural Health Education
- Nursing Consultants

- Newspapers & Magazines
- Nutrition
- Nursing Homes Equipment
- Nurseries
- New Business Consulting
- Nitrogen
- Nets & Netting
- Noise Control Products
- Newspaper Distributors
- New Thought Churches
- Natural Gas
- Newspaper Back Issues
- Newspaper & Print Advertising

O

- Oil Burners Services
- Ostriches, Rheas, & Emus
- Online Shopping Information
- Occupational Therapy & Rehabilitation
- Optical Goods Service
- Online Banking
- Oxygen Equipment
- Overhead Door Contractors
- On-Hold Music & Message Services
- Outdoor Benches
- Orthodox Churches
- Outboard Motors

- Ornamental Residential Iron Work
- Otolaryngology Physicians & Surgeons
- Oil & Gas Burners
- Oil Field Contractors
- Ornamental Aluminum Work
- Orthopedic Chairs
- Ornamental Metal Work
- Optical Disk & Imaging Equipment
- Outdoor Furniture
- Orthodox Synagogues
- Oil & Grease Seals
- Oil Field Transportation
- Overhead Doors - Commercial & Industrial
- Orchard Equipment
- Olive Oil Wholesale
- Orthopedic Appliances
- Online & Securities Trading
- Ostomy Equipment
- Organ Parts
- Office Supplies
- Office Movers & Relocators
- Orchestras, Symphonies, & Bands
- Online Correspondence Schools
- Opera
- Open Bible Churches
- Oil & Gas Field Services
- Oil Field Specialties

- Odor Elimination & Control Services
- Oral Surgeons
- Oriental Restaurants
- Orthopedic Shoes
- Office Supplies Delivery
- Outdoor Furniture Recovering & Repair
- Oil & Gas Companies
- Orthopedic Shoes Repair
- Outfitters & Guides
- Outdoor Kitchens
- Oil Burners - Commercial
- Oversize Loads Trucking
- Orthopedic Shoes Technicians
- Out-Reach Ministries
- Oxygen Equipment
- Office Furniture & Equipment
- Oral & Maxillofacial Pathology & Surgery Dentists
- Ornamental Iron Work
- Oriental Carpet & Rug
- Occupational Health Chiropractors
- Orthopedics Pediatrics Physicians & Surgeons
- Outdoor Advertising
- Oil Field Pumping Equipment
- Oil & Gas Attorneys
- Office Services
- Oil Field Equipment Repair
- Off Road Vehicle Parts, Supplies, & Accessories
- Overhead Doors
- Off Sale Liquor Stores
- Outerwear & Work Clothing
- Orthopedics Chiropractors
- Ophthalmology Pediatrics Physicians & Surgeons
- Oil Burner Equipment
- Oak Furniture
- Oyster Bars
- Outboard Motors Parts
- Outsourcing
- Orchard Services
- Ornamental Shrub & Tree Transplanting Services
- Outplacement Services
- Organ Donation & Tissue Banks
- Ornamental Plaster Moldings
- Ozone Equipment
- Occupational & Industrial Medicine Physicians
- Oncology Physicians
- Optometrists
- Oysters
- Office & Loft Buildings
- Office Furniture & Equipment
- Oil & Grease Absorbents & Removers

- Opticians
- Oil Well Testing
- Outdoor Sports Equipment
- Outdoor Lighting
- Organic Farms
- Oil & Gas Producers
- Organic Foods & Products
- Office Buildings & Parks
- Oil Reclaiming & Recovery
- Oncology Veterinarians
- Office Designers
- Outlet Malls
- Oil Handling Equipment
- Oil & Gas Consulting Services
- Optometry Information
- Oil & Gas Marketing
- Office Furniture & Equipment Refinishing & Repair
- O-Rings
- Office Trailer
- Ornamental Iron Work Supplies
- Off Road Vehicle
- Optometrists' Equipment
- Office Building & Industrial Cleaning Services
- Offset Reproductions & Printing
- Orthopedic Braces
- Oil Field Equipment
- Oriental Goods & Foods
- Osteopathic Physicians
- Oil & Gas Exploration
- Oil Well Services
- Otolaryngology Pediatrics Physicians
- Optical Goods
- Oil Refineries
- Optometry Clinics
- Oil Field Construction
- Organ Tuning & Repair
- Off-Track Betting
- Oil
- Outdoor Sports & Recreation
- Oil & Gas Well Drilling
- Office Automation Equipment & Systems
- Oxygen Therapy
- Online Shopping
- Ovens - Commercial
- Orthopedics Physicians
- Orthodontics Dentists
- Ophthalmology Veterinarians
- Osteoporosis Physicians
- Oriental Goods
- Orthoscopic Surgeons
- Oil & Gas Land Leases, Properties, & Royalties
- Ophthalmology Physicians
- Outplacement Consultants

- Occupational & Industrial Health & Safety
- Orchid Growers
- Osteoporosis Information
- Office Furniture & Equipment Installation
- Oil Spill Cleanup Contractors
- Omelet & Quiche Restaurants
- Orchards
- Oil Well Logging & Perforating
- Office Space
- Otology Physicians
- Orthopedics Podiatry Physicians & Surgeons

P

- Pet Food
- Packing & Crating Materials
- Pet Containment
- Pet Transportation Services
- Pipe & Boiler Covering Contractors
- Property Maintenance
- Podiatry Pediatrics Physicians & Surgeons
- Post Offices
- Party Facilities
- Pizza Equipment
- Printing Equipment
- Plastic Raw Materials

- Plastic Pipes
- Portable Stages & Platforms
- Poultry Equipment
- Pretzels
- Private Hunting Facilities
- Psychotherapists
- Puppet & Marionette Shows
- Printing Consultants
- Protective Covers & Cases
- Portable Storage
- Plastic Foam Products
- Private Schools
- Paralegal Schools
- Portrait Photographers
- Pharmaceutical Laboratories
- Party Equipment Sales
- Phone Equipment & Systems
- Piers
- Playhouses & Treehouses
- Parachutes
- Parking Facility Equipment
- Paternity Testing
- Plants & Trees Nurseries
- Pizza
- Photo Laboratories
- Psychic Consulting & Healing
- Pharmacists

- Phone Directory Advertising
- Production Painting Industrial
- Pinball Machine
- Projection Equipment
- Pet Grooming
- Product Safety Consultants
- Painting Equipment
- Police Departments
- Physical Therapists
- Prosthetic Eyes
- Peruvian Restaurants
- Plastic Extrusions
- Propane Gas Bottled & Bulk
- Photo & Scrapbooking Albums
- Pharmaceutical Products
- Plasters & Plastering Materials
- Preventive Medicine Veterinarians
- Phone Equipment & Systems
- Partitions & Dividers
- Petroleum Products
- Plastic Scrap
- Pet Clothing & Accessories
- Pasta & Pasta Machines
- Painting Contractors
- Pet Related Services
- Pipe & Boiler Covering Materials
- Physical Therapists Information
- Plastic Finishing & Decorating
- Parking
- Public Accountants
- Picnic Equipment
- Pre-stressed Concrete
- Physical & Biological Research - Commercial
- Proctology Physicians
- Private Tennis Courts
- Perfumes & Colognes
- Plasterers' Equipment
- Packaging & Shipping Services
- Portable Toilets
- Pens & Pencils
- Prototype & Tooling Machine Shops
- Piano Rolls & Discs
- Prosthetic & Artificial Limbs
- Purchasing Services
- Printing & Publishing
- Paint Spraying Equipment
- Private Detectives
- Photography Schools
- Public Address Systems
- Playground Equipment
- Photographic Equipment Service & Repair
- Plate Glass
- Pipes Cutting & Threading

- Paper & Plastic Bags
- Plumbing & Heating Supplies
- Portable Buildings
- Plastic Bag Sealers
- Professional Photographers
- Prepaid ATM Debit Cards
- Plotters Equipment
- Parks & Playgrounds
- Patio Equipment
- Personal Insurance
- Propane Gas Equipment
- Pressure Cleaning Services - Residential
- Process Service
- Psychologists
- Professional & Amateur Sports Teams
- Pager & Beeper Sales
- Pest Control Equipment Manufacturers
- Political Campaign Services
- Party Lighting
- Party Invitations & Announcements
- Precision Electronics Sheet Metal Fabrication
- Pension & Profit Sharing Plans
- Plumbing Contractors Information
- Public Health & Safety
- Printing Design Services
- Plastic Containers
- Personal Development Programs
- Potatoes Distributors
- Passenger Railroads
- Psychological Examiners
- Payroll Services & Systems
- Pneumatic Equipment Components
- Plasterers' Equipment Wholesale
- Plastic Cards
- Pest Control Services
- Pulleys & Sheaves
- Percolation Testing Laboratories
- Pumps & Extra Parts
- Public Speaking Schools
- Pest Control Equipment
- Patio & Sidewalk Cleaning Services
- Paintball Facilities
- Plastic Packaging
- Paperboard Boxes
- Pipeline Equipment
- Psychiatry Physicians
- Prosthetics
- Personal Computer Peripheral Equipment
- Plotting Services
- Printing & Writing Paper
- Paint Removal - Commercial
- Pesticides
- Pipe Coatings & Linings

- Parks & Recreation Consultants
- Plaster Craft Products
- Pedodontics Dentists
- Probation Services
- Plastic Custom Molding
- Pumping Contractors
- Poultry
- Photo Film Developing
- Pipe Fittings
- Petroleum Oils
- Postage Equipment & Service
- Presentation Graphics
- Primary Batteries
- Pediatrics Optometrists
- Pharmaceutical Containers
- Poultry Processing
- Public Golf Courses
- Plumbing & Heating Contractors
- Pins
- Public Administrators
- Preschools & Kindergartens
- Plastic & Plastic Products
- Publishers' Shipping Services
- Periodontics Dentists
- Pet Adoption
- Plate Glass Window Restoration & Sealing
- Physicians & Surgeons Information
- Persons with Disabilities Organizations
- Plants
- Personal Trainers
- Publishing Consultants
- Petroleum Oils Wholesale
- Photographic Color Prints & Transparencies
- Pharmacy & Pharmaceutical Consultants
- Playhouse & Treehouse Builders
- Plants & Trees Wholesale & Growers' Nurseries
- Pumps Service & Repair
- Pubs
- Potting Soil
- Photographic Art
- Paint
- Plumbing Equipment
- Pasta Restaurants
- Property Management
- Personal Watercraft Repair
- Public & Private Swimming Pools
- Paint - Commercial & Industrial
- Pictures & Prints
- Psychological Information
- Paper Towels
- Passport & Identification Photographers

- Pain Clinics
- Podiatrists' Equipment
- Prefabricated Metal Buildings Manufacturers
- Pilates
- Plating - Commercial
- Power Transmission Equipment Service & Repair
- Precious Metals
- Plasterers
- Pediatrics Physicians
- Podiatry Information
- Phone Directory & Guide Publishers
- Plastic Pipe
- Planters & Planter Boxes
- Physician Assistants
- Power Plant Equipment
- Plaques
- Pet Cemeteries
- Pharmaceutical Information
- Paint Stores
- Pest Control Services - Commercial & Industrial
- Plumbing Fixtures
- Photographic Equipment
- Plywood & Veneers
- Paintball
- Pet Shops
- Pet Memorials & Urns
- Powdered Metal Fabricators
- Puzzles

- Pet Waste Removal Services
- Picture Framing Supplies
- Poster Printing
- Personal Services
- Package Design
- Psychic Research Centers
- Photo Restoration & Preservation
- Picture Hanging Services
- Personal Financing
- Pony Rides
- Polyurethane Products Manufacturers
- Paving Consultants
- Protestant Churches
- Plastic Molders
- Pearls
- Pool Halls
- Paint Removal & Stripping
- Pharmaceutical Equipment
- Prescription Services
- Painting Contractors - Commercial & Industrial
- Photography Studios
- Phone Communications Services
- Plant
- Publishers' Representatives
- Perforated Metals & Plastics
- Process & Industrial Pipe

- Pregnancy Counseling & Information Services
- Piano & Organ Movers
- Pet Training
- Professional, Technical, & Trade Books Publications
- Parking Area Construction
- Poultry Wholesale
- Parking Services
- Parking Management
- Plumbing Service & Repair
- Parking Garages
- Public Fishing Lakes & Ponds
- Photogrammetrists
- Pianos & Organs
- Petroleum Consultants
- Plastic High Pressure Laminates
- Pave Stone Contractors
- Public Insurance Adjusters
- Postcards
- Pilots' Equipment
- Plastering, Drywall, & Insulation
- Paving Materials
- Plowing, Cultivating, & Rototilling Services
- Pet Breeders
- Pharmacies
- Printing Plates & Negatives
- Periodontal Prosthesis Dentists
- Personal Cell Phone Equipment
- Photographic Consultants
- Pillows
- Passport & Visa Services
- Party Favors
- Photographic Mounts
- Professional Organizers
- Picture Frames Restoration
- Pet Loss Counseling
- Packaging & Shipping Materials
- Portrait Studios
- Pianos
- Plastic Bags
- Party Equipment
- Petting Zoos
- Portable Showers
- Protective Coatings
- Piano Tuning, Repair,
- Physical Therapy Equipment
- Pneumatic Tools Repair
- Prefabricated & Modular Buildings
- Paving Stones
- Pipes & Smoking Accessories
- Pumps Installation
- Physical Therapy Equipment Repair

- Polygraph & Lie Detection Services
- Pathology Veterinarians
- Pressure & Chemical Cleaning Industrial
- Point of Sale Systems
- Paving Equipment
- Patent & Trademark Attorneys
- Portrait & Commercial Photography
- Pressure Cleaning
- Precious Metal Sheets, Wire, & Tubing
- Personal Escort Services
- Project Management
- Plate Glass Windows
- Patent Development & Marketing
- Preferred Provider Organizations
- Private Fishing Lakes & Ponds
- Product Development & Marketing
- Pet Enclosures & Runways
- Pools, Spas, & Hot Tubs
- Pet Care Services
- Plastering Contractors - Commercial & Industrial
- Private Racquetball Courts
- Pathology Physicians
- Print & Lithograph Inks
- Pipe Locating Service
- Personal Transcribing Services
- Pewter & Pewter ware
- Property & Casualty Insurance
- Public Stenographers
- Pulmonary & Respiratory Physicians
- Protective Eyewear
- Proofreading
- Philippine Restaurants
- Plastic Fabrics, Films, Rods, Tubes, & Sheets
- Pet Grooming Supplies
- Precious Metal Refiners
- Police Equipment
- Professional Engineers
- Personnel Management
- Poultry Hatcheries
- Pallet Trucks
- Paper & Distributors
- Physicians' & Surgeons' Answering Services
- Picnic Grounds & Services
- Pressure Vessels
- Pipelines & Pipeline Services
- Polyethylene Materials
- Psychiatric Hospitals
- Plastics Research
- Pollution Control Services
- Piano Instruction
- Porch Shades

- Picture Framing & Matting
- Pet Furniture
- Paper Products
- Patio, Porch, Deck, & Gazebo Builders
- Pneumatic Tools & Equipment
- Pipes & Tubes Bending, Cutting, & Fabricating
- Pain Management Dentists
- Plastic Lining Materials & Membranes
- Protective Coating Applicators
- Plumbing Equipment
- Potato Chips
- Pumps
- Pretzels Wholesale
- Parapsychologists
- Physicians & Surgeons Recruitment & Staffing
- Paper Towel Holders & Dispensers
- Plumbing Engineers
- Professional & Trade Associations
- Paper & Pressure Sensitive Labels
- Psychoanalysts
- Pet Medications
- Paint Removers
- Pajamas
- Pile Driving Machinery
- Probate Services
- Painting Consultants
- Paper Shredding Services
- Petroleum Testing Laboratories
- Pet Consultants
- Pocket Knives
- Printed Envelopes
- Parenting Information
- Photography
- Pulmonary & Respiratory Pediatrics
- Paper Shredding Machines
- Paper & Mill Representatives
- Plumbing, Drain, & Sewer Consultants
- Pet Cremation & Funeral Services
- Product Design
- Patent Searchers
- Pawn Shops
- Precision Springs
- Pet Insurance
- Pregnancy Clinics
- Printing Presses
- Portrait & Photographic Enlargement
- Property Law Attorneys
- Plastic, Metal, & Foil Labels
- Port Authorities
- Plant Shop Supplies
- Paper Shredding Machines Service & Repair

- Poultry Farms & Services
- Private Golf Clubs
- Public Affairs Consultants
- Photo Retouching & Coloring
- Prepress Services
- Portable Air Conditioners
- Pharmaceutical Research
- Plumbing Contractors - Commercial & Industrial
- Public Opinion Analysis
- Plastering Contractors
- Pizza Restaurants
- Paper Mills
- Plastic Fabrics, Film, Sheets, & Rods Manufacturers
- Payroll Transfer Agents
- Pipe Cleaning Equipment
- Periodical Publishers' Representatives
- Pottery
- Posters
- Pipe
- Phone Communications Services - Residential
- Private Duty Nurses
- Prefabricated Insulated Piping Systems
- Pickles & Pickle Products
- Pipe Thawing
- Piano
- Pile Driving Contractors
- Polynesian Restaurants
- Propane & Natural Gas
- Precast Concrete
- Pilot Car Services
- Pet Supplies Delivery Services
- Panels & Paneling
- Pavement Stripe Painters
- Pipeline Contractors
- Perfumes & Colognes Raw Materials
- Printing Ribbons
- Powder Processing & Coating Industrial
- Pizza Delivery
- Performing Arts Schools
- Plastic Injection Molding
- Pulpwood
- Paintball Equipment
- Party Decorating Services
- Parking & Traffic Consultants
- Psychic Arts & Sciences
- Pallets & Skids
- Private Golf Courses
- Proposal Services
- Physical Therapy Clinics
- Prefabricated Masonry Panels
- Packing & Unpacking Household Furnishings
- Parasails
- Packaging Containers
- Polygraph Examiners

- Plant & Fiber Products
- Payroll & Payroll Tax Preparation Services
- Pressure Cleaning Equipment
- Portable Swimming Pools
- Parks & Recreation Equipment
- Printed Circuit Boards
- Permanent Make Up
- Pay Phones
- Plastic Molds Manufacturers
- Power Presses
- Phone Cards
- Pre-Arranged Funeral Plans
- Pressure Washer Repair
- Pump
- Pork
- Printed Circuit Board Manufacturers
- Picture Frames
- Psychiatric Social Workers
- Poles
- Portable Sawmills
- Pharmacology Physicians
- Plating Consultants
- Personal Injury Attorneys
- Portable Welding
- Plumbing Contractors
- Popcorn Equipment

- Precision Grinding
- Pavement Marking & Striping Equipment
- Pipe Inspection Services
- Paralegal Services
- Pet Cemetery Equipment
- Party Decorations
- Pile Driving - Residential
- Payroll Distribution Services
- Pets & Animals Lost & Found Services
- Powder Coatings
- Patent Drafting Services
- Plastic Forming
- Public Utilities Consultants
- Propane Gas Service
- Plastic Blow Molding
- Popcorn & Popcorn Supplies
- Patent Agents
- Pipe Reconditioning
- Package Shipping Agents
- Podiums, Pulpits, & Lecterns
- Public Schools
- Printed Circuits Stamped & Etched
- Promotional Hot Air Balloons
- Podiatry Physicians
- Party Paper Goods
- Personal Loans

- Personal Financial Services
- Palm Readers
- Personalized License Plates
- Podiatry Clinics
- Printers' Support Services
- Packaging Machinery
- Pet Grooming Schools
- Pain Management Physicians & Surgeons
- Plastic Embedments
- Public Tennis Courts
- Propane Gas - Commercial
- Personnel Consultants
- Photo Albums
- Power Sweepers & Scrubbers
- Professional Employer Organizations
- Public Speakers
- Plants Wholesale
- Pediatrics Dentists
- Power Transmission Equipment
- Presbyterian Churches
- Portrait Painting
- Private Investigator Schools
- Physicians & Surgeons
- Pilots' Flight Information
- Personal Computer Printers
- Production Control Equipment & Systems
- Private Transportation Services
- Photo Laboratories - Commercial
- Psychic Life Readings
- Parasailing
- Pathology Laboratories
- Publishers
- Personal Secretarial Services
- Professional & Industrial Video Equipment & Systems
- Product Liability Law Attorneys
- Pre-hung Doors
- Paving Contractors
- Paper Mill Machinery
- Picture Frames Manufacturers' Supplies
- Personal Shopping Services
- Pancakes & Waffles Restaurants
- Pet Grooming & Boarding
- Prefabricated Steps
- Pails
- Phone System Consultants
- Porcelain Enamel Repair
- Performing Arts
- Paramedics
- Propane Gas Refilling Stations
- Phone Advertising
- Painting & Decorating

- Physical Therapy
- Private Tennis Clubs
- Plating Equipment
- Prefabricated Chimneys
- Prosthodontics Dentists
- Paper Tubes & Cores
- Photography Studio
- Plastic Machinery
- Pentecostal Churches
- Pottery Instruction
- Photographers - Commercial
- Personal Injury Referrals
- Party Entertainment
- Private Investigators
- Pastry Shops
- Party Games
- Phone Equipment & Systems Wiring & Installation
- Party Services
- Pest Control Information
- Product Development Engineers
- Packing & Crating
- Private Clubs
- Pavement Sealing
- Photofinishing
- Pharmacists' Temporary Help
- Photo Imaging
- Pipes, Tubes & Fittings
- Professional & Commercial Divers
- Physicians & Surgeons Clinics
- Power Plant Contractors
- Phone Equipment & Systems - Commercial
- Party Planning
- Product Packaging, Labeling, & Shipping
- Pneumatic Equipment
- Pet Sitting & Day Care
- Power Protection Systems
- Placement & Scholarship Bureaus
- Personal Watercraft Sales
- Pediatrics Surgeons
- Psychics & Mediums
- Propane Engine Conversion
- Print
- Putting Greens
- Porcelain Products
- Personal Watercraft Insurance
- Public Libraries
- Plumbing Equipment & Parts
- Photo Booth
- Piping Contractors
- Plastic Barrels & Drums
- Prosthetic Breasts
- Private Delivery Services
- Pet Rehabilitation Services
- Political Organizations
- Pipe Cleaning Service

- Printed Circuits Equipment
- Plastic & Transparent Boxes
- Polishes
- Pillow Renovating
- Portuguese Restaurants
- Parking Facilities
- Piano Parts
- Payroll Auditors
- Precast Concrete Form Erection Contractors
- Precision Tools
- Polyurethane Products
- Pavement & Parking Area Maintenance & Marking
- Photo Modeling Studios
- Piling
- Programmed Instruction
- Printing Services
- Pacemakers
- Pole & Post Frame Buildings
- Parochial Schools
- Property Tax Assessment Agents
- Patent & Proprietary Pharmaceuticals
- Plastic Compression Molding
- Phone Equipment & Systems Parts
- Printing Equipment Service & Repair

Q

- Quarries
- Quilting Machines
- Quality Control Consultants
- Quilting
- Quilting Materials Wholesale
- Quartz
- Quilts

R

- RV Appliance Service & Repair
- Range & Oven Parts
- Roofing Materials
- Retirement Living Information
- Rustic Furniture
- Rustproofing
- Rubber, Metal, & Plastic Stamps
- Recording Studios
- Restaurant Equipment Service & Repair
- Real Estate Attorneys
- Recycling Pick-Up Services
- Real Estate
- RV Cleaning
- Recycling Information & Training
- Refrigerant Reclaiming & Recycling Services
- Recreational Trails

- Roof & Wall Flashing
- Ribbons Manufacturers
- Roof Inspection Services
- Rehabilitation Centers
- Remodeling & Repair Contractors
- Radio Stations
- Radio Communication Equipment
- Real Estate Environmental Assessments
- RV & Campers
- Rodeos
- Range Hoods & Canopies
- Resume Services
- Refrigerators & Freezers - Commercial Sales & Service
- Rape Prevention
- Refrigeration & Air Conditioning Installation
- Ribbons
- Recreation & Sports Books
- Radio Parts
- Records Destruction
- Restaurant Interior Designers
- Restaurants Architects
- Radiator Covers & Enclosures
- Restaurant Equipment
- Restaurant Employment Agencies
- Racks Manufacturers
- Ready-Mixed Concrete
- Razors & Razor Blades
- Restaurant Management
- Refrigerating Service & Repair
- Roofing Equipment
- Refrigeration - Commercial
- Real Estate ' Supplies
- Rolling & Sliding Doors
- Roof Curbs
- Running Boards
- Recycled Paper & Cardboard
- Residential Care Facilities Information & Placement Services
- Radio Communication Systems & Services
- Radiation Physics Services
- Restroom Equipment, Supplies, & Service
- Remnants
- Riding Clothing & Equipment
- Real Estate Tax Search
- Roofing Contractors
- Railroad Ties
- Roof Coatings
- Radio Controlled Vehicles
- Race Car Parts & Equipment
- Robots & Robotic Systems
- Refrigeration Parts

- Railroad Contractors
- Radiation Testing & Inspection
- Reform Synagogues
- Roofing Shingles
- Rehabilitation Chiropractors
- Running & Jogging Supplies
- Retirement Benefits
- Rent to Own
- Road & Highway Contractors
- Raw Bar Restaurants
- Residential Maintenance
- Real Estate Investment Trusts
- Real Estate Title Search & Abstract Services
- Real Estate Advertisers
- Racquetball Equipment
- Recreational Trips & Guides
- Ringtones
- Real Estate Information
- Refrigeration Contractors
- Respite & Recovery Care
- Rifle & Pistol Ranges Equipment
- Radiology Veterinarians
- Roof Decks
- Residential Content Appraisers
- Room Additions
- Reformed Churches
- Religious Vestments
- Refrigerators & Freezers
- Real Estate Escrow Services
- Racing Engines
- Roofing Contractors Information
- Retirement Income Funds
- Restaurant Equipment
- RV & Camper Equipment & Parts
- Risk Management & Loss Control Insurance
- Railroad Maintenance
- Radio Paging Equipment
- Refrigeration
- Real Estate - Commercial
- Rust & Paint Removal
- Real Estate Agencies
- Rheumatology Pediatrics Physicians & Surgeons
- Radiotherapy
- Rheumatology Physicians
- Roofing Consultants
- Racquetball Clubs
- Roofing Hatches & Scuttles
- Refrigerator & Freezer Sales
- Roofing Maintenance & Repair
- Roof Structures & Trusses
- Rifle & Pistol Ranges

- Radios
- Religious Organizations
- Restaurant Insurance
- Restaurant Cleaning Services
- Recording Instruments
- Recycling Centers
- Real Estate Foreclosure Assistance & Services
- Retirement Communities & Homes
- Recycling Equipment Manufacturers
- Real Estate Auctioneers
- Roller Skating Rinks
- Roadside Assistance
- Real Estate Exchanges
- Radon Testing & Mitigation
- Religious Counseling Services
- Record Promotion
- Radiator Coolants & Solvents
- Resins
- Rooming & Boarding Houses
- Race Car
- Radar Equipment
- RVs
- Reinforced & Composite Plastic
- Religious Practitioners
- Retirement & Life Care Centers
- Radio Equipment
- Real Estate Agents
- Recreation Program Consultants
- Resale, Second Hand, & Used Merchandise Stores
- Rubber Manufacturers Supplies
- Rock & Lime Hauling
- Real Estate Investments
- Reiki
- Room Air Conditioners
- Ready & Custom Made Slip Covers
- Restaurants
- Radiology Chiropractors
- Recycling Consultants
- Racks
- Radio Sales & Service
- Roofing Equipment Service
- Research & Development Laboratories
- Religious Goods
- Retaining Walls Contractors
- Radiators - Industrial Rebuilding, Service & Repair
- Reforestation Service
- Retirement Apartments & Hotels
- Records Management
- Reweaving & Mending
- Retirement Housing

- Refrigerated Trucking
- Resident Cash Buyouts
- Real Estate Developers & Sub dividers
- Rape Treatment Centers
- Reunion Planners
- Roofing
- Rock Shops
- Repair & Remodeling Insurance
- Residential Care Facilities
- River Trips
- Recreation Centers
- Railings
- Retirement Planning Consultants & Services
- Retreat Facilities
- Residential Real Estate Attorneys
- Radio Station Equipment
- Road Surface Preparation
- Racquetball & Handball Courts
- Records Searchers
- Recruitment & Staffing Services
- Relocation Services - Residential
- Real Estate Buyer
- RV Transport
- Radiology Podiatry Physicians & Surgeons
- Refrigerator & Freezer Parts
- Recycling Services & Equipment
- Real Estate Support Services
- Radiant Heating & Cooling
- Reflexology
- Religious Education Schools
- Refrigerating Parts
- Recording Equipment
- Rubber & Plastic Stamp Equipment
- Real Estate Attorneys - Commercial & Industrial
- Recorded Dance Music
- Rock scaping
- Roofing Contractors - Commercial & Industrial
- Recruiters
- Raft Trips & Tours
- Repossession Services
- Reading Improvement Instruction
- Registered Master Plumbing Contractors
- Radio Broadcasting Consultants
- Road & Highway Construction Materials
- Rags
- Recorded & Live Information Services
- Radio Communications Equipment
- Real Estate Video Services

- Real Estate Schools
- Room Air Conditioners Service & Repair
- Raised Floors
- Road Treatment & Dust Control
- Real Estate Loans
- RV Insurance
- Rhinestones
- Record Labels
- Restaurant Food Products
- Retirement Housing Custom Blinds
- Road & Highway Construction Machinery & Equipment
- Real Estate Settlements
- Russian Restaurants
- Roof & Siding Cleaning Services
- Real Estate Buyer Consultants
- Reptiles
- Rehabilitation Services
- Rubber & Plastic Hose
- Radio Phone Equipment
- Religious Goods Stores
- Real Estate Loan Processing
- Recreation Areas
- Restaurant & Guides
- Restaurant Menus
- Reprographic Services
- Railroads
- Resorts & Vacation Cottages
- Range & Oven Sales & Service
- River Rock
- Radio Program Producers
- Rolling Mill Machinery
- Research & Development Services
- Recording Studio Equipment
- Repair Shops
- Registered Public Accountants
- Rubber Products
- Radiology Schools
- Radio Station Representatives
- Rivets
- Radiology Pediatrics Physicians & Surgeons
- Recycled Products
- Rhinology Physicians
- Rehabilitation Medicine Physicians & Surgeons
- Restaurant & Hotel Fixtures
- Real Estate Publications
- Research & Development Engineers
- Race Car Fabrication & Repair
- Risk Management Consultants
- Resorts Reservations

- Radio Advertising
- Reels
- Real Estate Appraisers
- Respiratory Therapy Equipment
- Rainwear
- Racquetball & Squash Courts Construction
- Refrigeration Equipment-Commercial
- RV & Camper Leasing
- Radiology Physicians
- Refractory Materials
- Respiratory Therapy
- Real Estate Consultants
- Rock & Stone
- Reverse Mortgages
- Relocation Services
- Real Estate Maintenance Protection Plans
- Rubber Stamps
- Recreational & Resort Properties
- RV Storage Equipment
- Rust Preventives & Removers
- Reproductive Endocrinology Physicians & Surgeons
- Riggers Equipment
- Real Estate Inspection Services
- Ropes, Twine, & Cordage

S

- Speakers
- Smoked Foods
- Sound & Video Recording Services
- Septic Tanks & Systems
- Social & Human Services
- Semiconductor Manufacturers
- Sportswear
- Sports Cards & Memorabilia
- Statuary
- Storage Sheds & Buildings
- Sales Promotions & Counseling Services
- Soil Testing
- Software Consultants
- Stretch & Shrink Film
- Stuffed Animals
- Service Stations
- Scarves
- Scenery Studios
- Security Guard Training
- Sand Industrial
- Sand & Gravel Hauling
- Seawalls Contractors
- Soap Dispensers
- Security Management Consultants
- Screen Printing
- Sex Therapy
- Siding Contractors - Commercial & Industrial

- Sports Consultants
- Street & Parking Lot Sweeping Services
- Sun Decks
- Signs Service & Repair
- Small Appliances Service
- Steeple & Spire Construction
- Satellite Television Equipment
- Stock Exchanges & Quotations
- Solar Energy Contractors
- Slip Covers
- Scanning Services
- Structural Steel Fabricators
- Sewer & Drain Pipes
- Sheet Metal Work - Residential
- Stainless Steel Pipes
- Sports Massage
- Scrap Film
- Shoppers' News & Guide Advertising
- Sanitary Landfills
- Surfboard
- Security Guard & Patrol Services
- Snow Removal - Commercial
- Sports Information & Reports
- Sawdust & Shavings
- Structural Steel Contractors
- Survival Schools & Instruction
- Specialty Movers
- Street Lighting Contractors
- Sclerotherapy Surgeons
- Saw
- Storks
- Sculptured & Acrylic Nails
- Sales Training
- State Courts
- Shower Doors & Enclosures
- Speech Aid Devices
- Steak & Seafood Restaurants
- Silverware
- Storage Batteries
- Speech & Hearing Information
- Spinologists
- Signs
- Scientists
- Satellite Television Equipment & Systems Service & Repair
- Strategic Planning & Forecast Consultants
- Sewer Construction Contractors
- Soda Fountain Shops
- Scales – Industrial & Commercial
- Sheet Metal
- Social Security Counselors

- Sign Installation & Hanging
- Sound Level Testing
- Suicide Prevention
- Surfboards & Surf wear
- Street Light Poles
- Slide Printing
- Sanding Machine
- Saw Mills Equipment
- Skateboards
- Sports & Entertainment Associations
- Sinks
- Smoking & Curing Services
- Sewer Locating Service
- Sewage Disposal Systems
- Spiritualists
- Safety Schools
- Security Equipment Repair
- Steamships
- Sheep & Goats
- Student Housing & Services
- Smoke Detection Equipment
- Shipping & Receiving Services
- Site Location Consultants
- Sports Medicine Physicians
- Soaps & Detergents
- Scissors & Shears
- Surplus Merchandise - Commercial & Industrial
- Surveyors
- Steel & Brass Stamp Manufacturers
- Slippers
- Specialty Printing
- Skateboard & Inline Skates
- Spices
- Sewing Schools
- Sports Agents
- Service Station Builders
- Skate Parks & Rinks
- Shipping Masters
- Specialty Animal Services
- Snow Making Equipment
- Salvadorian Restaurants
- Small Appliances
- Stone Setting Contractors - Residential
- Surety & Fidelity Bonds
- Security Doors & Windows
- Snoring Treatment
- Secretarial Employment Agencies
- Sailboats & Sailing Supplies
- Swings
- Septic Tanks & Systems Cleaning - Residential
- Skating Rinks Installation, Equipment,
- Screw Machine Products

- Stoves Service & Repair
- Senior Citizens' Products
- Ship Building & Repair Equipment
- Stools
- Solar Energy Designers
- Salvage Disposal
- Structural Steel Detailers
- Stainless Steel Fabricators
- Swimming Pools Water Delivery
- Swimming Pool Decks
- Scholarships & Financial Aid
- Safes & Vaults
- Shopping Centers & Malls
- Soaps & Detergents Manufacturers
- Stop Watches
- Surveying Instruments
- Skin Care Products
- Secretarial Services
- Sun Rooms, Greenhouses, Solariums, & Atriums Builders
- Shelter Associations
- Search Engine Marketing
- Surfing Instruction
- Steel Products
- Stage Lighting Equipment
- Stress Management Clinics
- Sweaters

- Specialty Warehousing
- Smokers Treatment Centers
- Speech & Hearing Clinics
- Shipyards
- Sports Psychologists
- Siding Refinishing & Repair
- Steel Wholesale
- Stucco & Coating Contractors - Commercial & Industrial
- School Bus Transportation
- Sewing Patterns
- Sanitation Consultants
- Satellite Communications
- Swimwear
- Special Needs Vehicle Conversion Services
- Storm Door & Window
- Seed & Grain Cleaning Equipment
- Seals, Gaskets, & Packing
- Soccer Facilities
- Silk Screen Printing
- Staircases, Stairs, & Railings
- Small Engines Repair
- Scales
- Shoe Stores Equipment
- Sporting Goods
- Special Education
- Sheet Music

- Silver Products
- Steak Restaurants
- Slot Machines
- Soul Food Restaurants
- Snorkeling
- Safes & Vaults Opening
- Slot Car Racing
- Septic Tank Cleaning & Pumping
- Soccer Clubs & Instruction
- Shrimp Wholesale
- Smog Abatement Consultants
- Scoreboards
- Synthetic Oils
- Shelving - Commercial
- Septic Tanks & Systems Consulting, Site Evaluation & Design
- Screw Machines
- Ski Lift & Ski Tow Equipment
- Sidewalk Cafes
- Swimming Pool Coping, Plastering, & Tiling
- Self Defense Schools & Programs
- Ship Painting
- Swimming Pools Service & Repair
- Softball Clubs
- Software & CD ROM Duplication Services
- Sewing
- Store Fronts
- Stainless Steel
- Sunroofs
- Steam Bath Equipment
- Scientific & Technical Consultants
- Swimming Pool & Spa Construction
- Social Clubs & Organizations
- Ski Tours
- Sewer Companies
- Soft Drinks
- Scissor Sharpening
- Soft Drinks & Mixers Wholesale
- Self Help Groups
- Survival Games
- Swimming Instruction
- Shelters
- Sound Proofing
- Schools for the Physically Challenged
- Sail Makers, Fabric, & Repairs
- Sports & Recreation Facilities
- Sewing Cabinets
- Sunglasses & Goggles
- Septic Systems - Commercial & Industrial
- Saw Blades & Handsaws
- Stairs
- Strapping & Strapping Equipment
- Stenciling & Designing
- Stocks & Bonds

- Smelters & Refiners Equipment
- Scalp Care & Products
- Self-Improvement & Motivational Schools
- Sports Bars
- Shutters
- Satellite Communications Downlinking & Up-linking
- Skiing Clubs & Organizations
- Sauna Baths
- Silks
- Seeds & Bulbs
- Shiatsu
- Savings Banks
- Scientific Instruments
- Septic Tanks & Systems Installation & Repair
- Stucco
- Stereo Equipment
- Specialty & Gourmet Foods
- Skate Shops
- Secretarial Schools
- Sexual Abuse Attorneys
- Sound Engineers
- Sand & Gravel
- Szechuan Restaurants
- Sewer & Water Contractors
- Shock Absorbers & Struts
- Shaved Ice

- Sewers & Drains Electrically Cleaned
- Sand Spreading Services
- Sign Equipment
- Sewer Equipment
- Steel Barrels & Drums
- Skating Equipment Wholesale
- Septic Tanks & Systems Contractors
- Satellite Dish Antennas
- Systems & Integration Engineers
- Space Planning
- Scuba & Skin Diving
- Scrap Iron & Metals
- Screen Manufacturer's Equipment
- Sewer Flooding Control Systems
- Sheet Metal Equipment
- Storage Racks
- Security Monitoring Equipment Wholesale
- Sewer & Drain Cleaning, Service & Repair
- Surgical Centers
- Shrimp
- Stationery
- Synthetic Rubber & Rubber Products
- Specialty Bags
- Social Security Consultants
- Shorthand Reporters
- Social Scientists

117

- Stair lifts
- Spa & Hot Tub
- Sweatshirts
- Survival Equipment
- Shake Roofing Maintenance
- Seventh Day Adventist Churches
- Staples, Staplers, & Tackers
- Snowmobiles
- Scaffolding & Aerial Lifts & Parts
- Sun Tanning Products
- Speech Correction Schools
- Siding Materials
- Sandblasting Equipment
- Sawmills
- Singing Telegrams
- Skydiving
- Specialty Stores
- Shirts
- Synthetic & Cultured Marble
- Saddlery & Harnesses
- Steel
- Snowmobile Trails & Facilities
- Shredded Paper
- Stone Cleaning & Restoration Contractors
- Sandblasting -Residential
- Sauna Equipment
- Salt
- Security Systems
- Sheet Metal Contractors
- Silverware Cleaning, Repairing, & Replating
- Southern Style Restaurants
- Stamp Collecting
- Spiritual Churches
- Sewer & Drain Cleaning Contractors
- Sun Lamps
- Software & CD ROM Production Services
- Sheet Metal Work Industrial
- Sicilian Restaurants
- Safe Deposit Boxes
- Sports Motivational Trainers
- Swimming Pools Installers
- Studios
- Shoe Shining
- Steel Processing
- Self Defense Equipment
- Stained & Leaded Glass
- Ship & Boat Parts & Accessories
- Stereo Installation & Repair
- Sales Organizations
- Snowmobile Parts
- Specialty Photographers
- Sleep Disorders Physicians
- Silversmiths & Goldsmiths
- Stock Yards

- Skin Protection
- Safety Glass
- Science & Nature Stores
- Snow blowers Service
- Store Fixtures
- Senior Citizens' Centers
- Soil Scientists
- Screen Houses & Enclosures
- Specialty Bookbinders
- Swimming Pools Management Services
- Social & Human Services Organizations
- Sports & Entertainment Centers
- Septic Tanks & Systems Inspection
- Septic Tank & Field Lines
- Surgical Instruments
- Snowmobile & ATV Parts
- Shower Curtains
- Stairs & Stairway Builders
- Sign Painting & Lettering
- Sewer Odor Detection
- Scottish & Irish Goods
- Steel Pipes & Tubes
- School Supplies & Equipment
- Skiing Equipment
- Stress Management Counseling
- Sewer Line Inspection
- Soil Engineers
- Strainers Industrial
- Soda Fountain Equipment
- Sample Cases, Cards & Books
- Staplers & Nailers
- Swimming Pools Remodeling & Renovation
- Stair Resurfacing
- Skiing & Snowboarding Instruction
- Semi-Private Golf Courses
- Specialty Advertising Agencies & Services
- Sanitary Engineers
- Sales Management Services
- Safety Clothing & Equipment
- Steel Fabrication
- Surgery Veterinarians
- Sewer Connections
- Snow Grooming Equipment Sales & Service
- Structural Integration
- Swimming Pool Equipment
- Staff Leasing Services
- Stadiums & Arenas
- Screen Printing Equipment
- Stenographic Court Reporters

119

- Soil Conditioners
- Surfboards
- Steel Distributors & Warehouses
- Sexually Transmitted Diseases Testing & Treatment
- Sales Presentations
- Springs
- Sports Club Managers & Promoters
- Social & Human Services Information
- Ship Cleaning
- Sports Vision Optometrists
- Spinning Wheels
- Sports Medicine Podiatry Physicians & Surgeons
- Souvenir & Novelty Shops
- Scales Repair
- Soil Conservation Services
- Stump Grinding
- Steel Bars, Sheets, & Strips
- Snow Removal & Sanding
- Scrap & Waste Materials
- Structural Engineers
- Shingles & Shakes
- Spas & Hot Tubs Equipment & Parts
- Sawmill Construction
- Speech & Hearing Specialists
- Savings & Loan Associations
- Snowmobile Tours
- Surgical Instruments
- Sandwich Shops
- Steam Cleaning - Commercial
- Sports Promoters & Managers
- Silicones & Silicone Products
- Screening & Sifting Equipment & Services
- Sand
- Ski Equipment
- Satellite Receivers
- Software Training
- Security Guard & Patrol Services - Residential
- Sodding & Sodding Services – Commercial
- School Bus Leasing
- Sushi Bars
- Silk Screen Printing Equipment
- Siding Material
- Souvenirs
- Sodding Farms & Sales
- Speakers Repair & Rebuild
- Slides & Film Strips
- Sidewalk Contractors
- Stairs & Stairway Builders - Residential

- Sports Facilities Construction & Contractors
- Sailboat Charter
- Saddlery & Harness Repair
- Synthetic & Blended Fabrics
- Security Systems & Services
- Shoe Shine Equipment
- Semiconductors & Equipment
- Speedometers
- Synthetic Lubricants
- Spas & Hot Tubs
- Speech-Language Pathologists
- School Psychologists
- Shipping Consultants
- Stock Photographers
- Support Groups
- Skating Clothing
- Steam Cleaning Services
- Steel Buildings
- Stone Setting Contractors
- Spill Control Equipment
- Ski Equipment Service
- Stucco Stone
- Sexual Abuse Counseling
- Stair Repair & Restoration
- Sewer Cleaning Equipment
- Small Animal Veterinarians
- Shoe Stores
- Special Coatings Painting
- Software Design & Development
- Sewage Treatment Equipment
- Sheet Metal Work
- Shopping Services
- Surveillance Equipment
- Sales Tax Consultants
- Steel Fabricators & Erectors
- Snow Melting Systems
- Sports Medicine Physical Therapists
- Ship Building & Repair
- Sewing Machines
- Spanish Speaking Churches
- Scientific Photographers
- Sausage Wholesale
- Shirts Repair
- Sports Medicine Chiropractors
- Social Security Attorneys
- Supper Clubs
- Small Appliance Parts
- Swimming Pool Covers
- Surge Protectors
- Sports Photographers
- Skylights & Solariums

- Semi-Precious & Synthetic Stones
- Sound Equipment & Systems
- Scanning & Plotting Equipment, Service,
- Store Designers & Planners
- Specialty Coatings
- Steam Cleaning Equipment
- Sewer System Inspection Service
- Sweeping Compounds
- Soccer Equipment
- Sewing Machine Parts
- Steam Traps & Specialties
- Shelving
- Soybeans & Soybean Products
- Sewing Machines Service
- Sandwiches
- Shoelaces
- Sound Equipment & Systems Repair
- Square Dance Clothing
- Security & Industrial Video Equipment
- Stress Management Psychologists
- Small Business Planning Attorneys
- Special Occasion Photography
- Service Station Equipment Installation
- Seafood Restaurants
- Swimming Pools Manufacturers & Distributors
- Singles Organizations
- Seamless Guttering
- Sewing Contractors
- Sexual Harassment Attorneys
- Snowshoes
- Stamps
- Smoke Abatement Equipment
- Siding Painting
- Semiconductors
- State Government Offices
- Swap Shops & Meets
- Snow Cones
- Sculptors & Sculptures
- Swimming Pool Enclosures Repair
- Shopping Carts, Baskets & Bags
- Shoe Repair
- Store Fixtures, Counters, & Showcases
- Spraying Equipment
- Sheet Metal Work Equipment
- Shooting & Target Ranges
- Satellite Equipment & System

- Sports & Recreation Clubs
- Steam Cleaning Equipment
- Salvage Yards
- Science of Mind Churches
- Satellite Television Antennas
- Satellite Equipment & Systems
- Sports & Entertainment Tickets
- Swimming Pool Enclosure Manufacturers
- Sculptors Equipment
- Stereo Equipment Custom Installation
- Skiing Guide Services
- Speech & Hearing Services Organizations
- Sound Effects
- Sanitary Products
- Salt Wholesale
- Showcase Manufacturers
- Stains
- Shuttle Transportation Services
- Stone Cutters
- Spa & Hot Tub Covers
- Safety Signs & Tags
- Snow Removal Equipment
- Sharpening Equipment & Stones
- Solar Energy Systems
- Screws
- Social Companion Services
- Septic Tanks & Systems Equipment
- Soil Consultants
- Storage Trailers & Containers
- Stained & Leaded Glass - Commercial
- Spanish Language Schools
- Sewer & Drain Cleaning Equipment
- Small Appliance
- Spinning & Weaving Instruction
- Schools for the Blind
- Sports & Fitness Instruction
- Shopping Cart & Basket Repair
- Self Service Laundries
- Snowboards Sales
- Skylights
- Specialty Meat Markets
- Solvents
- State-Certified Real Estate Appraisers
- Southeast Asian Restaurants
- Ski Resorts
- Speech & Hearing
- Special Design Machinery
- Spirit Filled Churches
- Spark Arrestors
- Speedometers Service

- Structural Steel
- Snowmobiles Repair
- Social Service Associations
- Skylights - Residential
- Security Equipment
- Soccer
- Sleep Disorders Information & Treatment Centers
- School Furniture & Equipment
- Shredders Manufacturers
- Special Interest Organizations
- Small Electrical Appliances Repair & Parts
- Social Security Services
- Spas & Hot Tubs
- Stamp Pads
- Self Service Moving & Storage
- Solid Waste Landfills
- Steel & Heavy Machinery Warehouses
- Sealers
- Sewer Contractors - Commercial & Industrial
- Street Cleaning Equipment
- Sports Medicine Equipment
- Saw Sales & Sharpening
- Sandblasting - Industrial
- Surveying Services

- Sewage Backup Cleaning Services
- Snow blowers
- Steel Joist Manufacturers
- Smoked & Dried Fish & Seafood
- Scrap Metal Buyers
- Sewage Plant Operation
- Special Transportation Services
- Satellite Television Services
- Siding Contractors
- Sports Camps
- Sausage
- Special Trades Contractors
- Sporting Goods Service
- Schools
- Skip Tracing
- Shuffleboards & Accessories
- Spa Builders
- Solar Energy Research, Design, & Development
- Slip Cover Fabrics
- Scale
- Soil Stabilization
- Skating Equipment Sales
- Smoothies
- Sexual Dysfunction Physicians & Surgeons
- Specialty & Fancy Boxes
- Sperm Banks
- SR-22 Insurance

- Stencils & Stenciling Supplies
- Suspended Ceilings
- Sexual Harassment Awareness & Prevention
- Security Consultants & Agencies
- Space Heaters
- Small Gas Engine Repair
- Serums & Vaccines
- Stereo Equipment Parts
- Seating
- Salads
- Spas & Hot Tubs Service
- Safe Experts
- Storm Shelter Contractors
- Smokestacks
- Synagogues & Temples
- Steam Generators
- Social Workers
- Spray Painting & Finishing
- Sewer & Street Water Engineers
- Speech & Language Consulting
- Soil Services
- Scaffolding
- Surgeons
- Seminaries
- Stationery Engraving & Imprinting
- Soldering Services
- Storm Doors & Windows
- Self Esteem Services
- Seasonings
- Stucco & Coating Contractors
- Stained Glass Schools
- Sandblasting
- Speech & Hearing Equipment
- Sound Systems Consultants
- Social Media Marketing
- Steel Mills
- SUV Parts & Service
- Shoe Dyeing
- Storm Door & Window Repair
- Schools for the Deaf
- Steam Pressure & Chemical Cleaning
- Swimming Pool Chemicals
- Security Cameras
- Speaker
- Searchlights & Floodlights
- Scrapbooking
- Scientific Instruments Service & Repair
- Sharpening Services
- Solid Surface Materials
- Sand & Gravel Handling Equipment
- Safe & Vault Movers
- Steam & Water Coils
- State Liquor Stores
- Safety Engineers

- Sewing Machine Parts, Supplies, & Attachments
- Stone Carving
- Southwestern Restaurants
- Soda Fountain Equipment Repair
- Swedenborgian Churches
- Shoring
- Sound Control Structures
- Sailing Instruction
- Squash Courts
- Sprinkler Supervisory Service
- Silos & Silo Equipment
- Sugar
- Sheet Metal Specialties
- Sewing Machines Industrial
- Spill Control Services
- Steps
- Sewing Machine
- Stained & Leaded Glass Manufacturers
- Surf Shops
- Sheltered Workshops
- Snowmobile Clothing
- Steel Straightening
- Sign Design Services
- Steel Detailers
- Snack Foods
- Soil Analysis & Testing Laboratories
- Surveys Industrial
- Sign Printing
- Seed & Grain Cleaning

- Sodding & Seeding Services
- Sheepskin Goods
- Smoke Odor Control
- Sign Engravers
- State Legislators
- Spanish Restaurants
- Skin Care Cosmetics
- Satellite Radio Equipment
- Sewage Treatment Consultants
- Steam Cleaning Equipment Repair
- Sales Employment Agencies

T

- Textiles
- Towing Equipment
- Thai Restaurants
- Tonneau Covers Service
- Truck Bodies
- Truck Tires
- T-Shirts
- Termite Control
- Tapestries
- Truck Repair Equipment
- Toys & Games
- Translators & Interpreters
- Tractor Equipment & Parts
- Tree Farms
- Tile Flooring

- Telecommunications Consultants
- Truck Transmissions
- Trademark Development & Searching
- Tobacco Buyers & Re-dryers
- Tennis Court Supplies, Resurfacing, & Repair
- Trucking Companies
- Tax Reporting Services
- Tank Truck Transportation
- Theater Tickets
- Technical Writers
- Trailer
- Toilet Partitions
- Tires
- Trucks - Commercial
- Tennis Clubs
- Textile Fibers Manufacturing
- Telegraph Services
- Truck Permits
- Tobacco Leaf Wholesale
- Traveler's Checks
- Toys Equipment
- Tourist Information & Attractions
- Truck Body Repair & Painting
- Trailer Transport
- Temperature Measuring Instruments
- Truck Bumpers & Tailgates
- Tank Installation & Removal
- Table Tennis Equipment
- Traditional Synagogues
- Thermometers
- Tables
- Tanning Beds
- Thread Rolling, Cutting, & Grinding
- Typesetting & Composition Equipment
- Trophies, Medals, & Awards Engravers
- Transportation Equipment
- Toll Booths
- Teleconferencing Equipment
- Trailers Service & Repair
- Travel Accessories
- Travel Wholesalers
- Tuckpointing & Cleaning
- Top Soil Manufacturers
- Transmissions & Parts
- Tennis Instruction
- Tanning Salon Equipment Repair
- Towing
- Trial Attorneys
- Theatrical Talent Inventory Services
- Towel Cabinets
- Tree Consultants
- Tree & Shrub Spraying

- Terrazzo, Marble, & Tile Contractors
- Towels
- Trucking & Shipping Inspecting & Surveying Services
- Tractors
- Telecommunications Equipment
- Telecommunications Equipment Service & Repair
- Theme Party Facilities
- Travel Medicine
- Talent Agencies & Casting Services
- Truck Bed Liners
- Tank
- Textile Painting
- Tanks Inspection & Testing
- Toy Stores
- Translators Equipment
- Tapas Bars
- Tanks
- Trophy Cabinets
- Tennis Racket Restringing
- Tanning Salons
- Travel Agencies Employment Agencies
- Timber Framing & Structures
- Television Tuner Repair
- Television Parts
- Truck Trailer
- Trade Clearing Exchanges
- Travel Emergency Assistance
- Theme Weddings
- Tax Grievance Services
- Trust Companies & Services
- Tanners Equipment
- Tree Fruits
- Truck Lube
- Tennis Clothes
- Travelogues
- Television Program Producers & Distributors
- Television Station Representatives
- Trampolines
- Television & Radio Advertising Production
- Tire Recycling & Disposal
- Toilets
- Tiles
- Tire Additives & Sealants
- Telecommunications Management Services
- Trademark Consultants
- & Searches
- Therapeutic Massage
- Taxi Services
- Tool Boxes & Tool Holders
- Travel Agencies Information

- Television & Radio Speakers Service & Repair
- Tropical Plants
- Taxis
- Tank Linings & Coatings
- Truck Trailer
- Thermocouples
- Technology Research
- Time Locks
- Telecommunications Employment Agencies
- Television Antennas
- Tank Cleaning & Draining
- Travel Industry
- Tax Sheltered Investments
- Theatrical Equipment Sales
- Truck Alignment, Frame & Axle Repair
- Theatrical Stage Sets Design
- Textile Machinery & Parts
- Transportation Contract Services
- Take Out
- Truck Caps & Tonneau Covers
- Tropical Fish Wholesale
- Table Cloths
- Tool & Alloy Steel
- Testing Equipment
- Textile Finishing Manufacturing
- Travel Consultants
- Tile Floor Contractors
- Tiaras
- Telecommunications Installation & Repair
- Truck Body
- Trailer Equipment & Parts - Commercial
- Tent Sales
- Tuxedos Sales
- Taverns
- Tree Trimming Services
- Transit Lines
- Topsoil & Fill Dirt
- Timber Cruisers
- Telemarketing Services
- Theatrical Stages
- Truck Leasing
- Tattoo Removal
- Technical Illustrations
- Taxation & Monetary Policy
- Traffic & Transportation Engineers
- Travel Medicine Physicians
- Timeshares
- Telecommunications Services
- Trade Commissions
- Textile Designers
- Taxidermy Equipment
- Teacher Associations
- Trailers

- Trophies, Medals, & Awards
- Taxicab Insurance
- Trailer Hitches
- Theatrical Managers & Producers
- Truck Refrigeration Equipment Service & Repair
- Time Clocks
- Truck Driver Leasing
- Tool & Machine Designers
- Televisions Parts
- Tire Patches
- Televisions Service & Repair
- Teleconferencing Services
- Trading Posts
- Tiles Contractors
- Tennis Courts Construction
- Tugboats & Towing
- Telemarketing Agencies
- Test Preparation & Tutoring Services
- Textiles Trimmings
- Tools
- Trucks
- Teen Clubs
- Tank Abandonment Services
- Travel Agents
- Toy Consultants
- Truck
- Truck Trailer Parking
- Theater Parties
- Tattoo & Piercing Equipment
- Tire Customizing
- Truck Equipment Parts
- Travel & Tourism Schools
- Telephone & Television Cable Contractors
- Taxidermy Instruction
- Tree Services - Commercial
- Table Tennis
- Tattoos
- Table Pads
- Tents
- Tool & Die Makers
- Tax Collectors
- Truck Engines
- Tortillas
- Tool & Utility Sheds
- Thermographers
- Truck Air Conditioning Equipment, Service & Repair
- Telecommunications Contractors
- Teeth Whitening
- Transcription Services
- Towers, Buildings, & Antennas
- Tempered Glass
- Tennis Court Surfacing Materials

- Tanning Salon Equipment
- Tennis Equipment
- Tax Return Preparation
- Tent Repair
- Thoracic Internal Medicine Physicians & Surgeons
- Tractors
- Television Program Services
- Television Service Providers
- Training Programs & Services
- Time Switches
- Toy Repairs
- Trucking Dispatchers
- Threaded Rods
- Tenant Screening
- Time Cards & Racks
- Tropical & Saltwater Fish
- Transfer Agents & Electronic Filing
- Textile Mills
- Traffic Ticket Dismissal
- Transportation & Public Utilities Law Attorneys
- Telecommunications Wiring & Cabling
- Tool & Die Makers Equipment
- Trailer Equipment & Parts
- Truck Beds
- Transplant Surgeons
- Thrift Stores
- Trenching Machines
- Truck & Van Customizing
- Tree Planting Kits
- Tabletops
- Temporary Housing
- Toxic Substances Attorneys
- Television Studio Equipment
- Tennis Courts
- Technical Translators & Interpreters
- Telemarketing Consultants
- Telecommunications Engineers
- Tube Fittings
- Trailers
- Tarpaulins
- Toilet Seats
- Tea
- Transportation Services
- Trailers - Commercial
- Toner Cartridge Refurbishing Services
- Tool Repair & Parts
- Tank Equipment
- Truck Ladders, Racks, & Boxes
- Tool Grinding
- Trademark Agents
- Typewriters
- Textile Printing Equipment

- Tool Designers
- Tennis Court Enclosures
- Trail Rides
- Trauma Surgeons
- Travel Insurance
- Time Stamps
- Tours & Charters
- Taps & Dies
- Teen Churches
- Toys
- Traffic Control Services
- Turbochargers
- Typewriter Supplies & Attachments
- Typing & Word Processing Services
- Truck Washing & Cleaning
- Travel Books & Maps
- Time Recorders
- Tubes & Tubing
- Truck Striping & Lettering
- TDD/TTY Telephone Services
- Truck Repair
- Tourism Consultants
- Taxidermists
- Telephone Services
- Truck Trailer Equipment
- Tree Services Equipment
- Textile
- Tax Return Preparation Accountants
- Traffic Schools
- Travel Marketing
- Truck Transport
- Television Stations
- Toning Salons
- Towing Information
- Theater Information Services
- Thrift & Loan Companies
- Tax Planning
- Taxicabs, Limousines, & Shuttles
- Testing Engineers
- Truck Insurance
- Table & Chair
- Tile
- Traffic Law Attorneys
- Trees
- Trap Skeet & Sporting Clay Ranges
- Tufting
- Tourist Homes
- Truck Parts & Equipment
- Tickings
- Turntable
- Taxicab
- Testing Laboratories
- Travelers Advisory Services
- Tunnels Construction
- Tablets Computers
- Tower Repairs
- Transportation Companies
- Television Advertising
- Trenching Contractors

- Tiles Refinishing & Cleaning
- Toner Cartridges
- Tax Publications
- Tank Disposal
- Tailors
- Two-Way Radio Sales
- Travel Clubs & Services
- Technical Manuals Preparation
- Trousers & Pants
- Tree & Stump Removal Services
- Televisions
- Titanium
- Tanks Maintenance & Repair
- Travel Training & Education
- Turbines
- Truck Trailers
- Thermostats
- Temp Agencies
- Title Insurance
- Tax Attorneys
- Time Management Training
- Theatrical Consultants
- Timber & Timberland Companies
- Truck Stops
- Tort Attorneys
- Truck Refrigeration Equipment
- TMJ Dentists
- Truck Storage

- Transit & Transportation Advertising
- Technical Service Engineers
- Trophy Shops
- Tax Consultants
- TV
- Traffic Reports
- Typewriter Repair
- Trampoline Centers
- Transportation Authorities
- Telecommunications Common Carriers
- Technical Writing Consultants
- Traffic Control Equipment
- Truck Washing & Cleaning Equipment
- Truck Driving Schools

U

- Upholstery Fabrics
- Used Machine Tool
- Underground Storage Tanks
- Used Furniture
- Used Washing Machines & Dryers
- Used & Waste Oils
- Used Trailers
- Used Refrigerators & Freezers
- Used & Rebuilt Marine Equipment

- Used Vacuum Cleaners
- Upholsterers' Equipment
- Used Restaurant Equipment
- Utility Trailers
- Used Sewing Machines
- Used Carpets & Rugs
- Urology Physician Referrals
- Uniform & Cleaning Service
- Used Small Appliances
- Used Pianos
- Underwear
- Umbrellas
- Used Mobile Homes
- Upholsterers
- Uniforms
- Ultraviolet Equipment
- Underwater Photographers
- Used Farm Equipment
- Used Photographic Equipment
- Used Buses
- Used Sporting Goods
- Used & Rare Magazines
- Used Store Fixtures
- Used Formal Wear
- Uninterruptible Power Supplies
- Used Clothing
- Unity Churches
- Used & Rebuilt Auto Parts

- Ultrasound Medical Imaging
- Used Tires
- Used Major Appliances
- Underground Wire & Cable Contractors
- Used & Rebuilt Motorcycles & Motor Scooters Parts
- Urology Physicians & Surgeons
- Used, Rare, & Out of Print Books
- Used Pipes
- Used Printing Equipment
- Urgent Care Centers
- Used Fur
- Utility Trailer
- Used Refrigerators & Industrial Freezers
- Unitarian Universalist Churches
- Used Musical Instruments
- Used Shoes
- Used Motorcycles & Motor Scooters
- Utilities
- Used & Rare CDs, Tapes & Records
- Used Cars
- Unfurnished Apartments
- Used Infant Clothing
- Unfinished Furniture
- Unlicensed Nurses
- Underground Conduit

- Used & Rebuilt Electric Motors
- Used Lawn Mowers
- United Church of Christ
- Used Barrels & Drums
- Used Silverware
- Used Office Furniture
- Used Appliances
- Used Cars Wholesale
- Used Scales
- Used Boxes
- Used Bicycles
- Underground Storage Tank Removal
- Used Brick
- Used Trucks
- Unemployment Insurance Consultants
- Used Stereo Equipment
- Uniforms & Accessories
- Urology Pediatrics Physicians & Surgeons
- Used Electric Equipment
- Underground Utilities Contractors
- Used Safes & Vaults
- Used Steel
- Used & Rebuilt Industrial Equipment
- Urban & Regional Planners
- Used Contractors' Equipment
- Upholsterers' Supplies Manufacturers
- Utility Location Services

- Used Tools
- Ultrasonic Testing Laboratories
- Used & Recycled Computers
- United Methodist Churches
- Upholstery Cleaning Equipment
- Used RVs
- Utility Contractors
- Used Restaurant Fixtures
- Uniforms - Commercial
- Used & Rebuilt Truck Equipment, Parts, & Accessories

V

- Vocal Music Instruction
- Van
- Veterinary Information
- Video Equipment Repair, Installation, & Repair
- Valet Parking
- Virtual Hosting Providers
- Voice Over Internet Protocol Equipment & Services
- Vitamins & Food Supplements
- Visual Training & Therapy Optometrists
- Video Equipment
- Vertical Blinds

- Vibration Measurement Equipment & Service
- Video Game Equipment
- Voice Response Systems
- Vault Doors
- Vacuum Cleaner Parts
- Videoconferencing Services
- Venture Capital
- Valves & Fittings
- Vinyl & Acrylic Windows
- Vietnamese Restaurants
- Vascular Medicine Physicians & Surgeons
- Veterans' Affairs
- Valves & Fittings Repair
- Videotape Advertising
- Violins
- Van Leasing
- Volleyball Clubs
- Voice Mail Equipment
- Volleyball Courts
- Vehicle Wraps
- Vinyl Flooring Manufacturing
- Venetian Blinds
- Vinyl Lettering
- Vacuum Cleaning Industrial
- Vapor Intrusion Testing & Mitigation
- Vacuum Pressure & Thermoforming Plastic
- Veterinary Schools
- Visual Arts
- Vending
- Videotape, CD & DVD Duplication Equipment & Systems
- Videotape Editing
- Vinyl Floor Installation
- Vehicular Accident Attorneys
- Vinyl Repair
- Vent Hood Cleaning
- Vending Machines
- Ventriloquists
- Veterinary Laboratories
- Vineyard Christian Fellowship Churches
- Video Games
- Vacuum Cleaning Systems
- Van Accessories
- Vacuum Cleaner
- Vocational Education
- Video Equipment
- Ventilating & Exhaust Fans
- Videoconferencing Equipment & Systems
- Vacation Packages
- Vending Machine Parts
- Video Consultants
- Variable Speed Drives
- Vinyl Doors & Windows
- Vacuum Deposition Coatings
- Veterinarians
- Vinyl Flooring
- Videography

- Voter Registration
- Vineyards
- Ventilating Contractors
- Veterinary Equipment
- Virtual Reality Game Equipment
- Video Gambling Machines
- Vacuum Cleaner Sales
- Video Production Services
- Virtual Offices & Assistants
- Virtual Reality Computer
- Vegetarian Food
- Vending Carts
- Vape Shops
- Voice Mail Business Systems & Services
- Vacuum Cleaners
- Variety Stores
- Vending Machine Merchandise
- Vinegar
- Volunteer Services
- Video Game Service & Repair
- Vegetarian Restaurants
- Villas
- Voice & Diction Improvement
- Vinyl Fences
- Vibration Control & Measurement
- Video Recorders Service & Repair
- Vacuum & Pressure Forming Plastic Manufacturers
- Vocational & Educational Test Publishers
- Vital Records Storage
- Vegetable Farms
- Video Arcades
- Vending Machines Service & Repair
- Vacuum Cleaning - Commercial & Industrial
- Ventilating Systems Cleaning
- Voice Mail Services
- Valances
- Vehicle License Services
- Voltage Regulators
- Van Conversions - Commercial
- Vacuum Cleaners Service & Repair
- Virus Removal
- Vacation Home
- Ventilating Equipment
- Video Cameras Sales, Service, & Repair
- Viatical & Senior Settlements
- Vacuum Cleaning Contractors
- Van & Truck Conversions
- Vocational Schools for the Mentally Challenged

W

- Wine & Distilled Beverages
- Wood Finishing, Repair, & Refinishing Services
- Women's Health Physicians
- Wall Decor
- Wheelchairs
- Weather Instruments
- Wigs & Hairpieces
- Wedding Dress Cleaning
- Water Pollution Control Equipment & Systems
- Welding Equipment
- Wood Preserving & Restoration
- Water Coolers
- Windstorm Insurance
- Water Analysis Equipment
- Water Extraction & Damage Restoration
- Welding - Commercial
- Wheels
- Weight Loss & Control Consultants
- Women's Accessories
- Wood Products Manufacturers
- Water Well Drilling Equipment
- Wedding Equipment
- Wood Windows
- Weight Control Centers
- Wine Accessories

- Wedding Caterers
- Water Pressure Cleaning Services, & Equipment
- Wholesale & Growers Nurseries
- Wire Cloth
- Woolen Fabrics
- Western Clothing
- Workers' Compensation Services
- Wood Chipping
- Waste Disposal Equipment
- Wood Blinds
- Weed Control Equipment
- Weight Loss Products
- Water Gardens - Commercial
- Wood Preservatives
- Wedding Dresses
- Wedding Candles
- Wildlife Environmental Services
- Watchmakers Equipment
- Water Softening & Conditioning Equipment
- Water Well Pumps & Tanks Service
- Weights
- Wood & Wood Products
- Windshield Wipers
- Workstations & Servers
- Water Gardens, Fountains & Ponds
- Water Sports Equipment

- Wedding Entertainment
- Water Well Drilling & Service - Commercial
- Wind Energy Systems
- Wallpaper Designers
- Water Consultants
- Wrecking & Demolition Contractors
- Water Well Abandonment Service
- Wedding Centerpieces
- Water Blasting Services
- WellPoint & Dewatering Systems
- Wall Coatings & Finishes
- Water Distillation Systems
- Warehouse Equipment
- Warehouses & Warehousing
- Water Trucks
- Waste Compactors - Commercial & Industrial
- Wastewater Management Industrial
- Washing Machine & Dryer
- Waterbeds
- Wildlife Removal & Relocation
- Writers
- Word Processing Employment Agencies
- Writing Services
- Water Treatment Chemicals

- Wagons & Carts
- Wines
- Wind chimes & Windsocks
- Wrongful Death Attorneys
- Wood Carvings
- Wood Doors
- Water Cooler & Fountain Repair
- Winches Industrial
- Web Sites
- Wallboard & Plasterboard
- Welding Equipment Repair
- Wallpaper & Wall covering Installation
- Water Mains & Water Works
- Wheels & Tires Service & Repair
- Weather Vanes
- Waste Paper
- Waste Management
- Well Drilling Equipment
- Whirlpool Bath Equipment
- Window Shades Equipment
- Weed Control Services
- Welding Inspections
- Window Contractors
- Welding Contractors
- Wastewater Treatment Engineers
- Water Hauling

- Water Skiing Instruction
- Wheelchair Lifts
- Wine Storage Equipment
- Wallpapers & Wall coverings Equipment
- Watches Service & Repair
- Winemaking Equipment
- Women's Crisis Intervention Services
- Water Heater Parts
- Wedding Cakes
- Welcome Services
- Wheelchair Lifts & Ramps - Commercial
- Waterfront Restaurants
- Wood & Laminate Flooring
- Winter Sports
- Water Blasting Equipment
- Wastewater Treatment & Disposal
- Wire & Wire Product Manufacturers
- Window Shades
- Wax
- Windmills
- Wholesale Laundries
- Water Heaters
- Wilderness Outfitters' - Guides & Tours
- Wildlife Refuges & Nature Preserves
- Women's Organizations
- Water Filtration Equipment

- Water Rights Surveyors
- Women's Shoes
- Waxing Hair Removal
- Women's Information
- Water Well Locating
- Waterproofing Materials
- Wedding Invitation Printing
- Women's Plus Size Clothing
- Woodcrafters Supplies
- Window Installation
- Wildlife Services
- Women's Clothing Contract Manufacturers
- Women's Clothing
- Wood Burning Furnaces
- Writing Schools
- Weigh Stations
- Water Purification Services
- Window Coverings
- Wrecker
- Whitewashing
- Waterproofing Contractors
- Wood Beams
- Wedding Gifts & Favors
- Web Design
- Water Jet Cutting
- Water Cooler & Fountains
- Water Resources Engineers
- Whistleblower Attorneys
- Water Conservation

- Wallpaper & Wall coverings Contractors
- Wrestling Instruction
- Water & Sewage Companies
- Wheel & Tire Balancing
- Waste Recycling Industrial
- Weddings
- Workers' Compensation Insurance
- Welding Equipment Manufacturers
- Wire Rope & Cable
- Waterbed Parts
- Water Works Equipment
- Wedding Planners
- Water Parks & Slides
- Window Shades - Commercial & Industrial
- Wiping Cloths
- Window Cleaning
- Water Treatment Service
- Walking Canes
- Wood Finishing & Graining
- Wooden Buildings
- Work Clothing
- Wallpaper Removing Equipment
- Wedding Flowers
- Wardrobes
- Wood Stairs
- Welding - Residential
- Wrongful Termination Attorneys
- Water Meter Inspection & Reading
- Waste Reduction Consultants
- Wireless Data Services
- Waste Treatment & Removal Services
- Wedding Chapels
- Wood Floor Refinishing & Resurfacing
- Wedding Venues
- Wakeboards & Equipment
- Washing Machine & Dryer Parts
- Wedding Attire Alterations & Tailoring
- Woodworking Equipment
- Wheels & Wheel Covers
- Wiring Cable
- Windsurfing & Kitesurfing
- Water Filtration Equipment - Commercial
- Water Treatment Systems
- Welding Rods
- West Indian Restaurants
- Women's Sportswear
- Word Processing Equipment Maintenance
- Washing Machines, Dryers & Ironers
- Water Well Drilling & Service
- Wood Finishing Supplies

- Water Utility Companies
- Watches
- Wedding Ceremonies
- Wood Pellets
- Whirlpool Baths Service
- Water Supply Engineers
- Work Gloves
- Water Skiing Equipment
- Weight Loss & Control Programs
- Wedding Invitations
- Water Well Inspection
- Wallpaper & Wall Coverings Installation
- Wedding Receptions & Parties
- Wood Carving & Turning
- Wooden Boxes
- Wineries Equipment
- Wood Waste & Recycling
- Wedding Dresses Dry Cleaners
- Weaving Equipment
- Wire & Wire Products
- Water Skiing
- Wedding Photographers
- Watch Bands
- Water Filters
- Wall & Ceiling Cleaning Services
- Wildlife Management
- Windows
- Water Transportation
- Web Hosting
- Weather Stripping
- Water Treatment Systems - Commercial & Industrial
- Weight Training Centers
- Welding Equipment
- Workers' Compensation Attorneys
- Wineries
- Weight Loss & Control
- Warehouse Distributors
- Warehouse Leasing
- Wedding Information
- Wedding Services
- Wedding Decoration Consultants
- Women's Underwear & Lingerie
- Window Tinting & Coating Materials
- Wireless Communications
- Water Softeners
- Wine Bars
- Wire Working
- Waste Paper Buyers
- Window Safety Film
- Window Shades Installation, Cleaning & Repair
- Water Sports
- Welding Repairs
- Warehouse Representatives
- Wastewater Control Equipment

- Window Coverings Installation, Cleaning, & Repair
- Wheelchair Repair
- Window Cleaning Equipment
- Water Heater Repair
- Windows & Parts
- Wheelchairs
- Waterbeds Service & Repair
- Web Conferencing
- Waste Compactors Service
- Window Glass Coating & Tinting
- Wholesale Distributors
- Wesleyan Churches
- Welding Services
- Window Repair & Replacement
- Wedding Tents
- Wildlife Rescue
- Water Sports Equipment
- Water Taxis
- Wine Consultants
- Word Churches
- Waste Disposal Industrial
- Woodworking
- Writing Consultants
- Wallpaper & Wall covering Removal
- Wall Units
- Wake-Up Call Services
- Women's Health Information
- Wetlands Consultants
- Web Site Developers
- Washing Machine & Dryer Repair
- Wedding Jewelry
- Weather & Meteorology Services
- Watchmen's Clocks & Systems
- Water Testing Laboratories
- Welding & Industrial Oxygen
- Window Cleaning - Commercial & Industrial
- Waste Management Equipment
- Wicker Furniture
- Wi-Fi Hotspots
- Women's Uniforms
- Welding Fittings
- Wedding Guides

X

- X-Ray Equipment Repair
- X-Ray Protection
- X-Ray Inspection Medical Laboratories
- X-Ray Duplicating Service

Y

- Youth Organizations, Centers, & Clubs
- Yoga Equipment
- Yacht Harbors
- Yarn
- Yacht Furnishings
- Yachting Clubs
- Yogurt
- Yard Signs
- Yoga
- Yacht Service & Repair
- Youth Services Organizations

Z

- Zoos
- Zippers
- Zoning Consultants
- Zinc